My Personal Walk and Talk with Jesus

LEE HOFFMAN

WestBow
PRESS
A DIVISION OF THOMAS NELSON

WestBow Press books may be ordered through booksellers or by contacting:

WestBow Press
A Division of Thomas Nelson
1663 Liberty Drive
Bloomington, IN 47403
www.westbowpress.com
1-(866) 928-1240

ISBN: 978-1-4497-1135-1 (sc)
ISBN: 978-1-4497-1134-4 (dj)
ISBN: 978-1-4497-1136-8 (e)

Library of Congress Control Number: 2011921057

Printed in the United States of America

WestBow Press rev. date: 03/03/2011

Introduction

As I was handwriting this book, trying not to forget some of the great miracles Jesus did that I was privileged to witness, I could feel and hear Jesus standing next to me, saying, "This is nothing compared to the Holy Bible."

He said, "I told my disciples what to write, and I am helping you to do the same, and if I don't, you are going to forget some of the things we shared together around the world." Jesus also mentioned he believed this book was going to be the best book since his Holy Bible, and I immediately asked him, "Why?" He came back with an answer I will never forget. Jesus said, "Because it is all about me." I told him it sure was, and I was proud to be there to see if all happen. I then asked Jesus if he thought it was one hundred times better. He said, "No, son, it is one thousand times better, except the Holy Bible."

I have always been taught never to doubt him, so I believe it will be the best because it is about the one who gave us our nose and our toes, and it is not fiction; it is all true.

From the time I was a young boy and able to read, if I knew a story was fiction, I wanted nothing to do with it. I asked myself why I would read about someone's imagination. I have my own imagination, and it is a lot better. God really instilled in me, "I want my children to learn the truth, and the truth shall set them free." I love that section of the Bible because it really helps God's children to have a much closer walk and talk with the Lord. I do not want all the blessings but would rather share them with God's children, young and old.

Thank you, my darling Lord Jesus, for your blessings, servant witness, and truth. In the back of the book, there is a special section where Jesus held my hand most of the time and told me many things he wanted his children to know and understand and not just think of as fables.

People are hungry to read about miracles they need. They are hungry to know that our Lord has already given an identical miracle to someone else. Do you agree? The main purpose for writing this book is to let you know you are not the first one with this problem, and if you or a loved one needs to have a miracle, then this may be the book you need to read.

Sign Painter

As sort of a tour guide, I had a sign painter paint the cover of the book when I was about seventy-two years of age. The artist told me to just draw it out, as I saw it in heaven, and he would paint it for me.

I did just that later and told Jesus, "I could have a fabulous artist redo it. Maybe it would look better."

"Wow," Jesus said. "Son, I like it just as it is. Don't change it or try to make it better."

I said, "You got it," and the more I see it, the better I like it.

I do not know where the sign painter is now, but I plan to invite him over for dinner with Jesus and me at my place in heaven; it will be a special day in my life and his, also.

Jesus and Me

Jesus does the healing, and I just do the praying. I consider myself as being the most privileged servant of the Most High. All I want to be is Jesus' sidekick. I love to brag about Jesus, the Son of the living God, and his miracles. Yes, I really thrive and just live for the opportunity to tell someone about him.

As I preached around the world and in different jails and prisons, I always started out my message by saying, "I can't heal a flea's headache, but I know the man who can, and his name is Jesus."

I have seen Jesus use my hands and shadow in miraculous ways to heal his children, and I am first to give Jesus all glory, honor, and praise. I believe the true miracle stories in this book and will try to tell you in every detail how they cannot only build your faith but also give you a better impression of the wonderful Jesus we have the privilege of serving and worshipping.

I believe reading about these miracles, as described here in their entirety, will be a much greater source of faith, guidance, and inspiration for you to rely on than all the books ever published in the world. They will tell you that your very own miracle is on the way, is coming, or that this is going to be your lucky day.

Read what your wonderful Jesus has already done for others and is more than willing to do for you, since him himself said, "I am no respecter of any person. What I have done for others I will do for you."

Praise the Lord.

Cover Story

On the cover, you will see me in my pajamas and my Lord and Savior, Jesus, walking the golden street of heaven. Jesus calls it paradise.

I don't want to explain too much here and now, but in the book, I go into complete detail about the entire trip with my precious Jesus—how I got there, all about the time Jesus and I spent together, and how I got back. It was fabulous to make the trip personally with Jesus.

Jesus said, "I never took anyone up to paradise this way and will never again." Read it carefully, and you will know the great difference and very personal way of going to paradise with Jesus and me.

This was not an accident but happened with a personal tour guide and was planned by the Lord Jesus himself. What a thrill and wonderful experience. *Wow!* I am very fortunate person and a privileged servant of the Most High. As you read it, I want you to believe it is really happening to you.

Praise the Lord.

I Go to Heaven

After the third night, I finally went to heaven. Yes, I have been in heaven and walked the gold streets with Jesus. The street are of gold, but they are transparent (you can look down through them like clear glass). They looked to be about twenty-five feet thick, just like its states in the Holy Bible in the book of Revelation. That's enough for now, but I will tell you exactly how it all happened. It is going to be very interesting, and I am not going to exaggerate one little bit, because the Lord Jesus would not like that one bit. He definitely would not approve of me, the servant of the Most High, not telling it 100 percent as it was. Following is the story in detail.

After the regular service I always have for the Lord, I was laying in bed but not asleep. I was just thinking about the Lord and how fortunate I have been to have such a wonderful relationship with Him when I noticed him standing on the right side of my bed. Jesus said in a soft, sweet voice, "Son, tonight thou shall be with me in paradise." I said, "Thanks, but not now," as I was finishing the planned World Healing Center; it is called "Jesus Miracle Chapel," and over 300 million people will drive past the big gold sign and the world's largest gold cross. It will be the world's largest structure of its kind.

I will also build the largest block glass cross in the world, all by myself. It is all lit up at night for the hundreds of millions of people to view. This is where I will talk to and counsel over nineteen hundred individuals on the beautiful porch that I will build, all by myself. I mention all of this because that is what I had in mind when I told Jesus, "Not tonight, but thanks anyway." He took my polite no and disappeared.

Jesus came back the next night after the regular service I always have for Him, and at the same time, as I was thinking about how fortunate I have been to have such a wonderful relationship with Jesus. He again said, "Son, tonight thou shall be with me in paradise," without being as emphatic this time. Again, I was thrilled and honored, but I again said, "No, I still want to build you the Jesus Miracle Chapel." He took my second refusal and disappeared as he did the night before. Wow, can you imagine this?

On the third night after the regular service I always have for the Lord, as I was again lying in bed but not asleep, I was just thinking about the Lord and how fortunate I have been to have such a wonderful relationship with Jesus. I noticed Jesus standing in the same place on the right side of my bed, and he repeated his request with a much more stern emphasis on the word *tonight*. I said, "Okay, whatever you say, my Lord."

Jesus picked me up in his arms, and I felt as light as a feather; away we went with a twinkle of an eye. The time passed, seeming like a second, and I was standing with my Savior on those transparent gold streets. As I have just mentioned, I want to tell you all about it, so I will try to cover all the things I had the privilege to see.

First, I might as well tell you, the tops of the buildings had large gold tops, and I think you call them onion domes. They were of very bright gold. The largest building was in the center, and I guessed it to be about twelve stories in height and made of very bright diamonds, each about the size of a large utility vehicle. On one side, there was a smaller buildup only half as tall of about six stories in height, which was made of rubies the size of the hood of a car and with a bright gold top. Both buildings were about three feet thick or a little more—maybe four feet thick.

The Bible says there are twelve pearly gates, three on four sides. I only saw four or five from where I was standing with Jesus. I always say, "If a lady has a pear ring she thinks, she has something great. Well, she hasn't seen anything until she sees the pearly gates." There is one large pearl for each gate. I would say they were over one hundred feet high. That is right, each pearl was one hundred feet high.

Holding the hand of Jesus, I was now standing right in front of him, no more than a foot or so apart. We are, I would say, of the same height. Looking Jesus right in his eyes with both of my hands on his shoulders, I shook him very gently and said, "Take me back home."

Now listen to Jesus' exact words. "You really want to go back, Son?"

At that time, I shook both of his shoulders a little harder and said, "Yes, yes, get me home."

Jesus said, "Okay, Son," and in his arms, he brought me back home and put me in my bed where he originally found me.

As I sit here now telling you my *Personal Walk and Talk with Jesus*, it seems like it was just last night. What a supreme privilege. I have heard people say they got into some kind of an accident with a truck or car or fell and ended up on an operating table and saw some white lights and thought they were in heaven. We have a few good Christian doctors who have even testified on television as to what their patients claimed when they woke up, and I am very happy for them that they had that wonderful experience. I still do not think that can compare with our Savior coming into my bedroom three nights in a row and actually asking me to take a personal trip with him.

Praise the Lord.

The Eastern Gates

The time before last when I visited Jerusalem, I was standing on the Mount of Olives looking down at what they call the Eastern or Golden Gate where Jesus will walk through. Probably millions of pictures have been taken of the famous gate. I promised myself the next time I came there, I was definitely going to go down and touch the gate, so I could say that before Jesus touches and walks through it, I put my hands all over it. This is sort of the way I think about the things that are most interesting and important things in my limited life on planet earth.

Well, here it is the next year, and here I am again looking down at the famous gate. In the front of that famous gate in a huge wall, there is an Arab cemetery with a fence around it. I walked down to the entrance of the cemetery where a guard gate is located. At this point, there is a guardhouse and two very large Arab soldiers standing at the gate of the cemetery. I walked up to them and told them I would like to walk through the cemetery. They were twice as large as me, and about six inches taller. They seemed like two guys you would not want to tangle with. They look at me eye-to-eye, and said, "Absolutely not," in a way that I knew they both meant it.

I don't really know if the large gold cross I wore on a gold chain around my neck hand anything to do with it, but I had made up my mind. That was the end of that nice thought, and I was just ready to say okay, turn around, and call it all off. Now, read very carefully.

9

There was Jesus standing in person. He was not a vision but in the flesh. He looked right into my eyes and said, "What do you want, Son?" Now, as I am writing this I am being very choked up, and a few tears are starting to come.

I did not call him Jesus. I just said I wanted to go through the cemetery and both guards said no, and I could not go. Jesus said to me, "Son, you go right ahead," and waved his hand for me to go. I thought, *Yeah, that is easy for you to say, but these two guys are twice my size, and they definitely said no.*

Jesus just smiled and said, "Go ahead," as he waved me on. I decided, *Okay, I will see what will happen if I go ahead.*

I walked right in front of the two guards. They were just about three feet in front of me, and I figured any second they would grab me by the neck and remind me that I could not go in. As I walked in front of the two, very, very, slowly, only, like I said, about three feet from them, I looked up at their faces, and it appeared they could not even see me. I looked at them, and they were staring ahead with glassy-looking eyes. I walked about four or five feet past them and then turned around again and looked at Jesus; yes, he was still standing next to them. He gave me a big smile and waved good-bye to me.

This story is going to get very interesting, as if it is not already. Walking through the cemetery along the wall for about five to six hundred feet, I came in front of the famous gate my Creator and Savior will soon be walking through. In front of the gate, there happens to be a picket steel fence of around nine feet high. The steel pickets are about four inches apart with sharp points on the top. Wow, I wanted to touch that gate, and I would have to climb over the very high steel points on the fence. I decided I had come this far and did not even consider stopping. I stood in front of the picket fence, and I climbed over to the top. Getting to the top, I put my legs over the points and dropped down to the ground and rolled over, so it would not be so hard on my knees, which were not so good at the time.

Now I was inside, and the gate was in front of me. The gate is made of heavy wood, and in the center are a couple of wood pieces across where the gates come together. Each side was about six feet wide and about seven feet high, made of heavy wood to hold the two gates together. I would say they are about eight feet long and about eight inches square, something like a wood-tie on a railroad. I was looking at this huge wood gate.

In a low voice to myself, I said, "I have walked all over Jerusalem in the steps where you have walked, and now you are going to walk in my steps." I walked in front of the gate taking baby steps all the way across, from one side all the way over to the other end, putting each foot right next to the other and saying, "You can't take a step without putting your foot where I have stepped." Then, I opened both hands and started to touch the big wooden gate.

I touched every single spot and said, "Now, Jesus, any place you touch this gate you will touch where I have laid my hands." Boy, did I feel good now. I had accomplished one of my greatest desires and dreams.

Inside of the gate grew some weeds with balls on them the size of, or just a hair smaller than, a golf ball. The balls had hundreds of little points coming from all around them, sticking out about an inch in all directions. They were a light cream-brown in color. I thought, *I would bet my friends would sure like one of these little balls from this special place.* I picked up five or six and stuffed them into my pants pocket and looked at that big, bright, steel fence about nine feet high and wondered how I ever got over it to get where I was now, or worse, how in the world would I ever get over it to get out of here.

I started to climb up, and as I did, I could feel all the spears from the round ball weed prick into my legs through my pants on both legs. I thought to myself, *This is nothing compared to what Jesus went through, so with his help, I will make it.* Well, I finally made it over the top and remembered, as I was putting both hands all over every spot on that gate, that I was speaking in many, many different tongues, or languages, but not a word of English. I walked down the street with my hand up in the air (as the Bible says to pray with your hands up) for about one and one and half miles back to the hotel where I stayed, and I was still praying in all those different strange tongues.

About seven years later, I thought, *What a dummy. I could have just passed the pointy weed balls through the steel pickets instead of in my pant pockets, and I need not get all those points picking me.*

Surely, this chapter will really interest the many millions of people who have taken a tour or trip to Israel the place called the Holy Land. I have been there myself many, many times, and every time has been wonderful and seemed more exciting than the last time. Undoubtedly, I could write

Coming out of Jesus' empty tomb.

A Talk with Michael the Archangel

Yes, what a privilege to have the Lord introduce you to the mighty angel Michael. I had a situation that kept coming up, and the vision kept making itself known to me. It was a vision of some demons. They were not bothering me, but I kept seeing them with this other person.

That night I went to bed and was saying my prayers after I had my service with Jesus, my love, as I always do. I was in the middle of my prayer when the Lord interrupted me and told me he wanted to introduce me to Michael, my archangel. I thanked the Lord very highly because I thought that was not only very wonderful but also a superior privilege. Wow, did Michael's voice come in loud and clear.

He introduced himself as Michael and told me he had already known about the situation. All I can figure out at this time is that the Lord must have explained the matter to him, as he knew all about it. Michael said, "I will completely erase that situation from your mind and it will never come back, and I will do it right now." As I was lying in bed, I could actually feel the whole matter leave my shoulders, I felt light as a feather, and he was right. It was gone forever. Thank you, Michael the archangel.

Now, for people who may not be too familiar with the power of Michael, He was sent to help Gabriel, the angel, out of trouble as the devil kept him in his power for a few days. Michael went to Gabriel's assistance to set him free so he could move on. I really want to thank the Lord for introducing me to Michael; I thought it was good to mention it to all my readers. The Lord, Michael, and I cannot wait to see you in person so we all can have a nice dinner with you. A Big Mac, large fries, and free senior drink come to mind.

Praise the Lord.

Controlled the Wind

I was reading the Bible during the night in my large family room. The room has about twenty or more windows. It was warm, so I had all of them open. All of a sudden, a very strong wind blew in, and all of the trees around the pool were actually bending. It was so noisy and windy as I was trying to read the Bible, and I could not keep my mind focused on what I was trying to read. It was getting worse and worse. I finally said, "Lord, I am really having trouble reading your words with all this noise and wind." The Lord asked me why I did not just tell the wind, and noise to just halt. I thought that was a clever idea, but I thought I did not have that kind of power. Then I thought, *Well, maybe if I did do in the name of Jesus, it will work.* I then said, "I take authority over you, wind, in the name of Jesus, and I command you to stop immediately." I am glad I used the world *immediately,* because in a heartbeat everything was so quiet you could hear yourself breathe. I mean, I never heard of such silence in all my life. I thanked the Lord and went on reading for another forty-five minutes or so. As I closed the Bible and thanked the Lord Jesus for giving me the authority in his name, the wind and noise immediately started up again at that second.

Lord, that was a real miracle, and I really appreciate you hearing me and answering my request. I believe the reason the Lord told me to talk to the wind was the he knew in his mind he wanted me to keep on reading his Holy words in the Bible. Thank you, Lord.

Praise the Lord.

Jesus Puts Five Fingers in Front of My Face

This story is a testimonial of what could be one of the greatest compliments the Lord could ever bestow upon one of his children.

He stood in front of me and told me that no one on planet earth had ever worked for him as diligently as I have. I honestly thought that he might be exaggerating. Out of curiosity, again I came up with a way, of course very diplomatic and humble in nature, to see why the Lord felt this way.

I spoke to the Lord in a gentle voice of the man named Noah, who spent over one hundred years doing God's work, namely, the building the ark. I believed that I had made my point in a very intelligent way, but what happens when you question your maker, going as far as to tell him he is mistaken? I will tell you know what happened to me.

My darling Lord put his very large hand, a hand that actually looks like mine, directly in front of my face, with his hand wide open, approximately ten inches in front of my face. He provided his answer. As he pointed to his five fingers in front of my face, there was *one* answer for each finger, starting with the pinky: emotionally, mentally, physically, spiritually, and the last, his thumb. It was truly a wonderful compliment. I cannot fathom anything better than when the Lord of Lords, and King of Kings, puts his large holy hand right in front of your face.

Thank you, Lord, I hope I can continue to up hold that great compliment.

Praise the Lord.

Chapter 2

Praying and Laying My Hands Way over a Million Different Individuals

Touch Over a Million

At the time of this writing, I figure I have laid my hands on over a million individuals and prayed for them. If I have my way, and I believe I will, if the *rapture* does not happen very soon, which I really hope it does, I hope I can have that number way, way up here at the Jesus Miracle Chapel that I have built mostly with my own hands. It could easily be another ten thousand people more every day. Boy, would that make me happy.

I am in pretty good health, thanks to the Lord, and that would even make me feel better. After I laid my hands on people around the world, in lines of twenty thousand or more, it really turns me on or peps me up, and I go away feeling younger and great.

This was on the front porch of the Jesus Miracle Chapel, as it was being built. I kept track, and it was over fifteen thousand. When I went up town to shop for groceries at some of the large supercenters, I always had people pull or drag me down an aisle and tell me they wanted me to pray for them or a loved one of theirs. We had figured that over a certain length of time are already well over twelve thousand. More, Lord, please, send me more.

Praise the Lord.

Knees Swollen Nail Goes Through

My knees have so many miles on them. That's the reason when my doctor sees my knee x-rays, he will say, "Boy, just looking at those x-rays really make my knees hurt." I used to dance on them almost every night for thirty-five years or more. Well, you want me to tell the truth don't you?

I carried tons of roofing and siding, for thirty-five years, and the final touch was when I built the Jesus Miracle Chapel. I carried thousands of heavy cement blocks—well, I mean tons—in my trusty wheelbarrow. That really helped do in the knees, as well as the ladder climbing; they say that will really do you in. I have climbed a twenty-four-foot extension ladder thousands of times with large tile pieces of roofing material on my shoulders and then a few thousand times when I alone built the world's largest glass cross trimmed on both sides with marble. My knees really hurt at times because the cartilage between my knee bones is completely gone. Therefore, when I walk, the bones are riding on bones, with no cushion left between them. I guess is that by now you are ready for the knee miracle.

Here it goes. Just before I started to build the Jesus Miracle Chapel, my left knee started to swell up. A few days earlier, a good knee doctor put a big needle in it and drew out about a half cup of water. In two days, it swelled up to three times its normal size. My neighbor saw it, because I had on a pair of white shorts. When she saw it, she told me she had never seen anything that large, and that it looked like a small watermelon. I told her, "I guess I will have to get on my knees and pray that it will go down tonight." She told me I had better sit in a chair and pray for it.

That night, I got down beside my bed on my bad knees and prayed that the swelling would go away during the night. In the morning, I believe it even was a little bit larger. I got out of bed and said, "Lord, I am not giving up." I got down on those very sore knees while I could barely bend, having loads of pain. I then started to talk to the Lord and told him when he was hanging on the cross with nails in his hands and feet, I knew it surely must have hurt a lot more than this, and I just knelt on my knees and continued to praise the Lord. After about three minutes on my knees, and telling Jesus how much I love him, this is what happened. I had a vision and could feel the nail, and at the same time in the very rear, I could actually see a huge nail spike and large hammer driving it through this swelled up left knee. It took the hammer about seven long hits before I could see the spike come through to the other side.

When the nail had gone all the way through, the huge knee was completely down to normal size, and both knees were the same. I was so happy and grateful, I jumped up and down on it and ran out of the bedroom to my family room, where I have a piano, a nice organ, and a special electric keyboard. I sat down at my keyboard and played the piece I love to play, "As the Saints Coming Marching In." I must have played it twenty-five times and sang as loud as I could, while pounding my left foot on the floor. My knee felt like a million bucks. I then jumped on my racing bike and drove as hard and fast as I could, shouting and praising my Lord Jesus, pumping as hard as I could. That knee felt okay for a long time until I started to carry all the cement blocks and wheel all that heavy cement and cement tiles. That gradually wore out the rest of the cartilage, but it was the most wonderful experience the Lord had blessed me with.

I will never forget, and I know my Lord knows where to get more praise, and I just keep thanking him and praising him until he gets darn ready to fix them. Boy, have I some good healing to look forward to.

Praise the Lord.

World's Largest Glass Cross
Designed by Rev. Lee Hoffman

After Hurricane Charlie

Jesus Stands by Me as I Eat Raisin Bran

I live in a trailer next to the Jesus Miracle Chapel, and on this particular morning, I was in my little breakfast room eating my raisin bran. I did not know that outside my window there were two men peering through my window. Going about my business eating my cereal, unexpectedly around twenty feet away from the breakfast room, Jesus appeared in the flesh (not a vision). Jesus walked over to me, put his hands on my shoulder, and sat right by me as I was eating. Jesus then looked over at the two men peering in the window. The two men were so shocked they fell over backward. It was the Lord's power. I thanked Jesus for coming over to have a special breakfast with me. The two men came to and knocked on my door. They were as white as a ghost and said to me, "You are surely a man of God; this is the most wonderful, exciting thing we have ever seen." What a true remarkable miracle this was for not only me, but also the two men who had the pleasure and honor to witness this miracle. They will have the power of the Lord in their hearts. Thank you, my darling Jesus

Praise the Lord.

Jesus Gets Man out of Bed to Bring Me a Wonderful Offering

I was on my way to town in my car, driving out the exit of the large circle driveway at the chapel. As I got out to the highway and started to leave my car stopped, it would not go in any gear. I tried them all, and it would not even move. This had been a wonderful car, and I had never had any problems with it since I bought it. I looked up and seen a car coming into the entrance of the large circle driveway. I got out of my car and went over to see who it was. It was a man all alone, and I said hello.

We walked up to the porch and sat down. I figured he had stopped in for a prayer. As we started to talk, he explained why he was there. These are his exact words: "I was sleeping real good when the Lord Jesus came into my bedroom, woke me up, and said to me, 'Get dressed, get into your car, and drive to St. Cloud. Drive down highway 192 and you will see my name, Jesus, in gold on the world's largest gold sign. Drive in and give the pastor there $1,000,' so here is a check for the thousand, and it's good."

I thanked him and prayed over the money. I never expected an offering for the chapel without praying for it and asking in return to give it back a hundredfold. The young man went into details of why he was led here. His name is Milton, and from that day forward, I never go to bed without praying for him and his family. I also every Christmas send him and family a wonderful card.

He said his good-byes, and I did say a nice prayer for him, and he was gone. I then walked back to my car, got in, and started it up. I put it in gear, and my car worked perfectly, like the day I bought it.

The Lord came to me and said, "Son, you almost messed up. If I had not messed up your transmission, you would have missed Milton and your blessing in a wink of an eye." Wow, Jesus you sure do know all about transmissions. I drove that car for about two and half more years, and it ran perfectly. Oh and yes, Milton drove 150 miles to find me and the large gold Jesus sign. What a wonderful Jesus we have to love and worship.

Praise the Lord.

You Are Welcome To take Pictures Of
The World's Largest Gold Cross
World's Largest Gold Jesus Sign
World's Largest Glass Cross

Over 1 Million Have From All Over the World

PRAYER OF SALVATION FOR ETERNAL LIFE.
LORD JESUS, I REPENT OF MY SINS. FORGIVE ME.
I CONFESS YOU AS MY LORD AND SAVIOR AND
BELIEVE THAT GOD HAS RAISED YOU FROM
THE DEAD.

COME INTO MY HEART AND CHANGE MY LIFE.
I THANK YOU, JESUS, FOR MY DYING SINS.

AFTER CONFESSING, THIS PRAYER, AND
BELIEVING WITH YOUR HEART, JESUS WILL
SAVE YOU.

**Drop In For Prayer
And
Miracles**

Chapter 3

Watching Jesus Take out Tumors in Brains and Stomachs and Heal Multiple Sclerosis, Blind Eyes, Cancer, AIDS, and So Much More

Gold Dome in Jerusalem

Phone Rings

I was standing in the living room right next to the kitchen; Jesus was in front of me. Jesus put both of his thumbs in both of my forearms and pressed so I would really know and feel it. Jesus said, "Get the phone," and the phone rang. I answered the phone, and on the other end was the Greater Miami Hospital. They told me they heard I pray for people; I said, "Yes, that is what I do." They then asked me if I could come down to the hospital, they had two people there that they wanted me to pray for.

I told them I would do my best to make the trip the next day, and I asked what the room numbers were. I did not know how they heard about me, and I did not ask. I just kept saying to myself that the Lord does work his wonders.

The next morning, I started out for Miami, which is I suppose about a hundred or so miles from where my home was in Boca Raton. Talk about raining; it reminded me of that old saying, "It's raining cats, and dogs," and that is what I had said to myself.

I had no idea where the hospital was, but I have the habit of always asking people. I finally found it, and I parked in the parking garage across the street on the fifth floor. I then walked across the street, went in, and asked the front desk woman where the rooms were. I cannot remember the numbers now, but one of them does stick in my mind as clear as if it were yesterday—407

In the meantime, I said to myself, *Lee, let us get going and see what this was all about.* I went to the first room. The door was open, and a few nurses, one or more doctors, and the mother of the ill boy were in the room. The boy was in one of those moveable beds, with wheels on the bottom. The boy lay there still, not moving at all. I introduced myself to the mother and doctor. I then had asked what was wrong. They mentioned the boy was in a real bad accident, and had glass somewhere in his head and was unconscious. I said, "What if I walked around in your bed. Wouldn't that be fun?

The child shook his head up and down. This movement startled the doctor, for the first time, and he asked me if I had witnessed it too. I replied, "Sure, he knows what I'm talking about." I was amazed with what we all saw. The mother had fifteen pictures of her son on a board on the side of the wall. I almost forgot to mention this, but they were all Spanish, and I did not have an interpreter there to talk with the mother. As for the boy, the Lord reminded me that he understood, and will understand you even though he does not speak any English. The Lord said, "Son, you saw how he moved his head. Therefore, he understood your every word." I thanked my dear Lord for reminding me of this. I had asked the interpreter to ask the boy's mother if I could have a picture to take with me so I could pray over it all night. The mother reached in her purse and showed me several more photos of her son, so I picked the one with him wearing a shiny light grey suit. He looked to be about five-foot-ten. I still to this day have that picture.

Back to the story; you may never be the same.

After giving the appropriate greeting good-byes, I took the picture home with me. It still was raining on my long drive back home. I did sing the whole way there and back to Jesus of how much I love him. This made the time go by much easier.

Finally, back home, I went straight to my bedroom and lay down on a beautiful pink cover, the same pink cover I will bring up later in the book. I took the boy's picture out of my pocket and laid it on my forehead, and before I could even start to say a prayer for him, my darling Jesus walked into the room, stood at the side of the bed, and picked me up in his arms about three feet high off my bed. When he picked me up, as he has done on several occasions, the Lord told me to go back to the hospital the next day and pray for the boy again. What do you say when your creator turns in a request like that? Um, you do as he says. When the Lord Jesus tells you, you have better do as he requests. Do not make up any type of an excuse. As I was so grateful, even to the Lord's voice, I agreed to do his wish. The Lord did not even lay me back down in my bed; he tossed me into the center.

I went back to the hospital as Jesus had asked, and the little boy was sitting in a chair, laughing, and playing. The doctor said, "When you left the little boy last night, he got up and was playing and laughing, and there is no glass at all in his head." The time the boy got up was the same time Jesus came to me in my bed and told me to go back and pray for the little boy. What a true blessing.

Now I have told this story to many people, and most of them say, "You told me there were two people in the hospital they called about for you to pray for." They all remember the other person and want to know. I tell you, it does my heart good to know that you were all listening.

Well, this is what happened when I went to the second room. There was a sweet little boy, about five years of age. He was sitting on the bed with his father, and his mother was sitting in a chair close to the door. I had a bottle of anointing oil with me, and I would have liked to put it on his little forehead in the form of the cross. I thought they might think I was a witchdoctor, so I kept it in my pocket. I walked over to the little fellow who was sitting on the bed with his dad. The Lord told me to touch him. I thought to myself, *How?* Jesus said, "Pat him on the top of his head, and tells him he is such a nice little boy." Therefore, I went over, gave him my best smile, and told him what a nice little boy he was. All the time I was patting him on his head, I said, "Jesus and I love you, and you are going to feel just wonderful. The father sitting on the bed was so nice and grateful and thanked me for coming down to pray for his son. We exchanged a few nice words. I told him not to worry about his son, as for he will be just fine.

Wow, I almost forgot to tell you the little boy's problem. I am sure he had two or three kinds of cancer. I can remember one begin leukemia.

As I walked to the door to leave, the mother had a grumpy look on her face, and she just nodded to me, and never even said thanks. I would never expect a good Christian woman to take such an attitude. I am no judge, but it sure looked to me as some kind of a cult. I do hope that I am completely wrong, but she could have at least said a few kind words.

In about two or three days, I did receive a call from the hospital. They said that they were happy to tell me there was no trace at all of any cancer. It looked as though he never even had it. Thank you, my darling Lord Jesus the healer. When you set out to do a job, you get the job done. What a truly remarkable blessing for those young boys.

As I sit here writing this story, I looked at the clock, and it was about 2:30 AM, just in time for me to start my big service as I do every night with Jesus, my love.

I might as well mention as I wrote this story, I was really living it, just as if it were yesterday. I will just call them tears of joy and thankfulness.

Praise the Lord.

Slammed Car

I was going to Pensacola for a revival for a few days, and I was driving my very large Pace Arrow motor home. On the rear was a very heavy steel carrier for my motorcycle. I always had my motorcycle so I could ride around town instead of driving my motor home. I pulled up to a fast food place to get a bite to eat. I thanked everyone and got back into my Pace Arrow. Unbeknownst to me, a new red vehicle had pulled up behind me. I put the Pace Arrow in reverse and backed up, and next thing I knew, I heard a very loud crash. I looked into my rearview mirror and saw I had hit the red vehicle on the entire right side. I pulled forward. The vehicle must have been about a foot and a half off the pavement. I thought, *Oh Lord, what did I just do?*

Sitting in the fast food restaurant were three guys, and it was their car. They came tearing out of the place screaming, "Oh my God, you almost mowed our car over." I jumped out, and told them, "Yes, I am so very sorry. It is all my fault, and I will pay for all damages."

Between the steel bumper and my heavy steel rack on the rear of my motor home, it was like a train on the railroad tracks. Seeing as I hit the right side of their car, I expected to see it completely smashed in.

The three men and I went over to see it, and the men just kept saying, "You almost tipped it over." As we looked at the side, there was not even one little dent. The men ran their fingers over the whole side and could not believe their eyes. I did not even knock the dust off it. The men kept rubbing it and kept saying they just could not believe it. None of us could believe it. I think I could hear the bank about a block away.

I was going to do the Lord's work, and the Lord sure looked after me. No wonder I love to do work for you, Lord. Thanks again. You sure saved me a lot of time and money. What a wonderful protector.

Praise the Lord.

Pace Arrow Motor Home
Traveled the United States Giving Away Bibles
Rev. Lee Hoffman

Red Pop

How does a bottle of red pop soda turn into a great miracle? Well, I will tell it just as it happened. It stills seem like it was yesterday. I was in my family room reading my Bible, and I knew I had a large bottle of red pop, but also I knew it was warm. I went out to the kitchen and thought if I put it in the freezer and leave it there for a spell, it would get cold faster, and it would be better than having ice cubes in it.

I went back to reading my Bible and got interested in some Christian television. After quite some time, I remembered I had put the large bottle of red pop in the freezer; I knew it would be very cold now. I walked over, opened the freezer door, and took out the glass bottle. Yes, this bottle was real glass, not plastic. Now I have to admit, I can see I did the wrong thing, but I wanted to see if it was completely frozen. I held it up to the light above my head with my face and eyes as close as I could get, and I would say I was eight or nine inches away from it.

It happened in a heartbeat and the blink of an eye. The big glass bottle exploded right in my face with my eyes wide open. The red pop bottle exploded in a hundred pieces, and with such force, the pieces were implanted into my wood cabinet doors. There was red pop all over the ceiling and a big puddle on the floor. The eight-foot mirror behind me had looked as though I threw a pail of red paint on it.

I figured I had glass in my eyes, red pop all over my face, white shirt, and white shorts, plus I was very worried about my eyes. I really thought I might have had a lot of sharp glass in my eyes. I ran into the bathroom on the same floor close by. I could not wait to turn on the light as I looked in the mirror. I was really expecting to see the contents of the large bottle of pop all over my face, hair, and white clothes.

Now here comes the miracle: there was not a drop on me, not even one little itsy bitsy drip on my hair, shirt, shorts, legs, nothing, and no glass in my eyes at all. I just could not believe that with the force of the bottle exploding the way it did, I did not have a drop of it on me. It just did not make any sense to me.

Then I heard the Lord say, "You cannot find one red drop, can you, Son?" I told the Lord, "You sure do have things under control, and I mean every little drop." Thank you, my darling Lord. I truly love and honor you, your grateful servant.

Praise the Lord.

Six Kisses

He looked to me to be in his late fifties, a very tall and very nicely dressed black man who came to the chapel. He could hardly walk and was bent over, looking very sick. He told me he had AIDS that was in the late stage and said he would be dead very soon.

If he were younger, he would have made a great basketball player. He was about a foot taller than me, and I'm six feet tall. I looked up at him and asked him if he loved Jesus. He could hardly mumble, but the words came out, "Yes, I do." At that very moment, Jesus said to me very clearly, "Kiss him six times on the neck and I will heal him." Now even though he was so tall and bent over, I still had to reach up and bring his head down so I could kiss him. Just as my Jesus had instructed me to do, I brought him down to my level, and as Jesus told me, I kissed his neck six times. He was very polite and thanked me and walked away just the same as he had come. I know when my master says he is going to do it, it really will be done. There was no doubt whatsoever in my mind.

It was two or three days later when he came back like a new man. He pulled up and he was just jumping, shouting, and kicking his heels, saying aloud, *"No AIDS!"* The hospital took more tests and found not even a trace of AIDS.

Now I have told this story to at least a couple hundred times to different people. I think a lot more people than that—yes, many more. I always stood up when I told the story, and I would throw in a little two-step of my own, to make it just a little more interesting. Since this is the first time I have written this miracle, the punch line does not go over as well. The man was very grateful and said, "You saved my life." I told him, "I just did the kissing. Jesus did the healing."

My pay is the blessing I get for bragging about the one and only true healer, my Jesus. Yes that is the same blessing I have received for well over the million people I have laid my hands on and was so privileged to see and witness the many miracles for so many years. Thank you, Lord Jesus, I will keep on kissing them, and you heal them.

We all know that Jesus did the healing the way he looked and the way he talked, and even admitted his short time to live. I honestly believe it would have happened very soon, even if the three of us had not gotten together as we did—the nice man, myself, and of course, our healer, Lord Jesus.

I also might mention, I told Jesus many do not have arms or legs. Jesus always comes back with the right answer, "If they don't have arms or legs, kiss them on the neck. It will be just the same." He mentioned I have lots of experience doing just that and that I must have kissed at least twenty-five thousand women and twenty-five thousand men on the neck and witness many miracles when I did so.

Yes, in the Holy Bible, it is requested that we kiss our brother with a holy kiss; it has been mentioned at least three times.

Praise the Lord.

Heals Boy's Deafness

I think this is a very important story of healing deaf people. It should help all preachers, priests, and rabbis, as well as all other people who pray for God's deaf children and expect results.

Another preacher and I held a small revival of only a couple of days at a high school. Probably about a thousand people were there, but as I remember, more miracles were there for a small crowd. It seemed like everyone received a miracle after the service.

We all went out into the lobby of the high school, and they brought up to me a very handsome black boy, about twenty-one years of age. They told me he was completely deaf; he could not hear a single word. Now the crowd saw so many miracles in the service when I touched them that when they brought the nice-looking young man over to me, they all said, "Heal him, Heal him." I cannot really blame them after seeing so many miracles take place. The crowd thought it was going to be easy. I right away, as I always do, told all the folks that I would do the praying, but only Lord Jesus can do the healing. This is one of my favorite sayings: "Lord Jesus does the healing; I do the praying."

I put my hands on his left shoulder, and said, "In the name of Jesus, ears open up and hear." Then I went behind him very closely, and said in his ear, "I love Jesus, I love Jesus," but he did not say anything at all, because he still could not hear me. Then Lord Jesus spoke to me so very clearly,

"Son, you cannot heal him. You are just praying over deaf spirits. You must cast out the deaf spirits first."

Is not Jesus wonderful? He even tells you to do it if you really expect it to work or happen. Therefore, I said, "In the name of Jesus, I cast out all the deaf spirits." I did not see the deaf spirits come out; I sure hoped and prayed that they did. Then I went behind him, but not so very close this time, and said in an ever-so-low voice, "I love fried chicken." As soon as I said that, he said out loud, and everyone could hear him, "I love fried chicken too." We all got a good laugh out of that, but I received a good token of praise. He gave me a huge hug and the two people on each side of him. I guess his friends then all gave me a hug. That is the way I have always wanted to receive my thanks and gratitude.

Thank you, my darling Jesus, for instructing your faithful servant as on how it should be done.

Praise the Lord.

Blossom of Faith

One year I went to Jerusalem with Paul and Jan Crouch with a wonderful group. As we always did, we visited all the popular places. One of them was the upper room where Jesus took the Lord's supper. As we were all standing there, two fellows brought a girl over to me who could hardly move. She had aluminum braces on both arms but still needed the assistance of the men on each side of her. They were about twenty-five to thirty-five feet away from me. I was standing alone, and they led her over to me. I did not ask them to, and to this day, why they picked me out of the crowd and brought her in front of me, I do not know. They asked me to pray for her.

Maybe it was the Holy Spirit leading them to me. I was quite surprised. I told them it would be a pleasure. I do not know why, but I opened my large right hand and laid it on her chest, and in the next second, my large left hand in the middle of her back. I pressed both hands on her back and chest. I could actually feel her grow about two inches right in my hands. I cannot remember the actual words I had said, but it was probably something like this. "Jesus we love you, and want you to heal our sister. She loves you, and we will thank you in advance." It was probably something like that, as I had said thousands of times before. The girl then threw off the aluminum braces and started to jump like a young cheerleader.

Do not stop now; it is going to keep getting better. We all got on the tour bus, and our next stop was to plant a tree. Paying $10 gives you a little tree, about ten to twelve inches high, to plant. We had to walk up the steps of a muddy hill, and I mean a soft, muddy climb. The girl asked me if she could go with me. There must have been about fifty on the big bus. I thought it was going to be a big step climbing up this soft mud and wondered whether she could make it. She indicated that since I had just healed her, she knew there would be no trouble. I told her not to say that. It was the Lord doing the work, and he had just used me as his tool to do his work. She realized she worded it wrong, and then up, up we went. This was a very steep hill, and she was climbing much better than I was. We all made it to the top, praise the Lord.

We dug a little hole, planted the tree on the side of the hill, and walked down, which was no easy task. When we got down, she and everyone had about three pounds of mud on each foot. I remember as if it was yesterday. We went to the outside rear of the bus, and then I cleaned off all the thick mud on her shoes. Two hours earlier, the girl could hardly take a step, and now she had just climbed a steep, soft, muddy hill. She gave me a big hug and kiss on the neck, and I was more than paid in full. After that, every night, as we sat and had a wonderful dinner in the main dining room, on the large tables with the white tablecloths, and which seated six people, she would always come over to my table, put her hand on my shoulder, kiss me on the neck, and thank me. She is still walking like a teenage cheerleader.

Praise the Lord. Last Supper Hand Carved

The Tile Lady

When I lived in Boca Rotan, I met a nice lady who had a tile store. She was a beautiful dark-haired lady, but her face was much distorted. She could only talk out of the side of her mouth.

I got to know her very well, and we talked quite a bit. She said that her face had been like this all her life, so she just tried to make the best of it. One time I was talking to her, and she asked me if I could do her a favor. "Yes. Yes, anything," I answered.

"Well, you see, my husband is in the hospital, and I had told him about you, and he was wondering if you could go to him."

I went to the hospital to pray for him, and he was a nice man. The next day, I went back to see the tile lady and told her I went to the hospital to see and pray for her husband. Now can you imagine this? When I looked at this lady, to my surprise, her face was completely normal. She was around forty years old, and for forty years, her face was distorted. She said to me, "When you were at the hospital talking with my husband, my whole face turned around. My husband said that he really likes you, and he can tell by looking in your eyes that you are an honest man, and that you have been touched by our Lord." I was eight to ten miles away praying for her husband, and the Lord did such a beautiful miracle on this young lady. He just decided that while I was at the hospital praying for her husband, he would show me another miracle healing in this beautiful lady. Well, he did show me.

Praise the Lord.

Grandma's Lost Mind

After a very successful revival meeting in Pensacola, Florida, the crowd had all left, and I was in my large motor home, ready to leave for home. I heard a loud knock at the door. I was the only one left, it was dark in the parking lot, and you have to be very careful. I grabbed my .38 pistol, went to the door, and said through the door, "Who is it, and what you want?" The voice came back, "We have our grandma here, and we had hoped reverend so-and-so (who was the preacher with me) would pray for her." When I heard the call of the other preacher's name, I felt a bit safer, so I held my gun behind me and opened the door. There stood two very tall large fellows with big beards.

They drove a 1957 Chrysler Sedan and opened the rear door, and pointed to their grandma. They told me she was completely out of her mind, and they hoped I pray for her that she may get her mind back. I told them to let me get my oil, and I would be right back. I grabbed a big bottle of oil and jumped in the back seat of their car.

I had never seen anything like this. She was waving her arms around in the air, and her mouth was going on and on, which did not stop. All that came out of her mouth was jabber, and the words made no sense. I took my index finger and put a few drops of oil on it and made the sign of the cross on her forehead. I was praying the entire time, and it seemed to make no difference at all. It was like praying for a telephone pole. I even tried to pray in different languages, but nothing at that time seemed to work. I said to myself, "Well, this just is not working." I wondered if I needed to use more oil, the way

Mosses did on his brother Aaron. I asked one of the men sitting in the front seat what in the world had gotten their grandma in such a state of mind.

This is exactly what he said to me: "About eight or nine months ago, she really started to worship the pope, and soon after that, she completely lost her mind and has never been the same." I thought to myself once again, *I bet I need to use more oil.* I poured out a handful this time and rubbed it all over her forehead. Wow still no difference. Well at this point, it's time to make a deal with the Lord. I said, "Lord Jesus, if you bring her back to her senses, I will sit here with her and pray until daybreak."

I did not hear the Lord say it was a deal, but I was still willing to stay with her until daybreak. I had been praying for forty-five minutes now. That's a long time to pray, but I was determined. I grabbed the large bottle of oil I had, and I started to pour it all over her head. I used the entire bottle of oil. There was so much oil on her and in her hair that I could have cooked up tons of chicken. Oil was running down her hair onto her nice black lace dress, but at this point, I was even more determined to heal her.

Now after about twenty more minutes of praying, wow what a miracle; she snapped right out of it. It was like nothing ever happened, and she was completely different. I had asked her to tell me that she loves Jesus, she replied very softly, "Well, I do love Jesus." Then I said, "Now tell me you love me." She answered, "Well, I love you." I thought I would see if she could combine the two, so I said, "Tell me you love Jesus and me." She said so nice and intelligibly, "I love Jesus, and I love you." I told her I would be paid for this in full right on the job. I said, "You owe me a big hug and a big kiss on the neck. That is payment in full." She agreed to that deal. She grabbed me and put her arms around me and gave me a big kiss on the neck about a half dozen times and did not want to let go.

Therefore, this is my oil story, and I had just as much oil on me as she did. I turned to the men, and said, "See Grandma? She is just like us now. Please, no more worshiping the pope." They promised no more worshipping the pope and that they would pray to Jesus.

I would like to thank our wonderful Lord Jesus for another well-done miracle and for me not stopping or giving up on her. Folks, praying really does make a difference. Just believe.

Praise the Lord.

Eyes Healed

If this happened today, I would not be writing this story, but it is a beautiful miracle from our wonderful Jesus, with a little different twist, so I really want to include it.

It happened probably about eleven years ago, and I know that technology has improved so greatly. That is the reason I mentioned this miracle. This very nice woman brought her young son to the chapel, and the three of us sat on the front porch to pray. I was building the chapel at the time, but when folks stopped to pray, I gave them my undivided attention.

The young boy looked to be about six or seven years of age. I could easily see that the boy's right eye was in a shape I have never seen before. His eye was actually hanging out of his socket, and it appeared to be hanging on his cheek. Lord, it was such a bad sight to see this little boy in this type of shape.

His mother said she had taken him to an eye specialist and that they told her they were afraid to do anything for the fear they might upset the optical nerves. Therefore, she decided to bring him to the chapel and ask me to pray in hopes his eyeball would be healed.

As I started to pray for him and his right eye, I was looking down, but my eyes were open. A veil, or I will call it a curtain, came over my right eye, and I could not see a thing out of my right eye. After I finished praying for the little boy, I raised my head, the veil was lifted, and I could see again.

As his mother and I looked at her son, *wow!* What a miracle—his eye was completely normal. After the three of us were done praising Lord Jesus for a beautiful miracle, his mother reached in her purse and handed me a $20 bill. I handed it back to her at least twice and said, "It gives me honor and pleasure to witness and pray for wonderful miracles. You see, to me, that is more than enough payment."

After all was said and done, the Lord Jesus in a very clear voice said, "Son, take her twenty-dollar bill." I thanked the nice woman and told her, "I accept the money, but I want you to know that it will go toward my electric bill, so I may keep the lights shining on the gold cross for all to see." She was very pleased when I told her this.

Yes, when my Lord Jesus tells me to do this or that, you can bet I am going to be obedient and listen. I know in my heart and spirit the Lord had a big blessing for her.

Praise the Lord.

Kenneth Hagan Revival

I enjoy going to other preachers' gatherings to see what is going on. I try to arrive early. It gives me the opportunity to mix and mingle with others and to say a prayer with them. Before the meeting had even started, I witnessed many, many miracles.

Let me tell you of this spectacular one. I was the very first to enter the large auditorium. It probably held a couple of thousand people or so. I walked in and was the only person in this large place. I picked any seat I wanted, so I headed to the very center of the building, and there I sat alone.

The next person to enter was a middle-aged man with a very attractive young woman who was pushing him in a wheelchair. I later found out that this young woman was the man's daughter, and I estimated her to be in her thirties. She pushed her father down the aisle to the center but stayed to the side.

We were still the only people in this large place with all the empty seats surrounding us. As I sat there by myself, the Lord Jesus directed me in spirit to go over and pray for him. I thought, *Okay, Lord, I am on my way over.* I walked over to them and felt quite at ease because we were in a place where people come to praise the Lord, also looking for healings. I stood by them and said, "I guess we are early," and I continued to chitchat.

After a little getting to know each other, and complimenting the daughter on how well she handles a wheelchair, I gave them the big question. "How long has it been since your dad has walked?" They both told me that it had been nearly eight years. Just as they told me that, the Lord of miracles told me very clearly to kiss him on the neck and said, "I will heal him right now." Boy, do I love to hear that, because when he says it, there is no doubt; it will be done. I told the man that the Lord wanted to heal him. I also told him, "The Lord would like me to give you the holy kiss on your neck."

Father and daughter smiled and told me it would be fine. I leaned over and kissed him three times on the neck. What a miracle; with my own eyes, I watched him jump out of his wheelchair, push it to the side door, pick it up in the air, toss it into the back of a large van, and walk back in to sit with his daughter.

I was so happy that I had arrived at the revival early to have such a fabulous miracle take place. I later, toward the end of the revival, watched the father with his daughter, and he could not have been more thankful to have such a wonderful miracle happen to him.

The Lord Jesus has used me to perform such magical, wonderful, and fabulous miracles. What a wonderful Lord we have.

Thank you, Lord Jesus, for allowing me, your brother Lee, to be involved in your wonderful work. Love to my Master.

Praise the Lord.

Better Gas Mileage

When I am done praying for people here, I always ask the Lord to give them better gas mileage. Here now in the United States, and all around, there is a serious gas price hike. When I am done with my prayer with the folks who come to see me, I always ask them to get three and a half or four more miles to the gallon. The folks usually end up laughing because I would end the prayer by asking the Lord to give them better gas mileage.

This is why, and when I tell them and you the story, you will understand. I had a big Pace Arrow motor home. It slept about eight people; there was a shower in the bathroom just like a home on wheels. There were two big gas tanks. One held about 30 gallons and the other 125 gallons. I am in Florida in Boca Raton, and I wanted to drive up to my hometown in Michigan. I filled both gas tanks up and headed toward Michigan. I was watching the gas gauge as it went down a half tank then a quarter as I was approaching Michigan. I looked back down at the gas gauge, and it was just on the top of empty. I thought, *Well, any minute I could switch over to my other gas tank.* I said, "Lord I think we are getting better gas mileage then we are supposed to. I am only supposed to get nine miles to the gallon on this thing." Then I said the magic words, "Well, with God all things are possible." Well, the gauge started to rise; it went from empty to quarter then half, all the way to full. The Lord put 125 gallons of gas back into the vehicle. I arrived in Michigan, which is around 1,350 miles from Boca Raton, with a full tank of gas. Amen.

I was telling an older woman this story, and she said, "I know you are telling the truth."

I looked at her and said, "I am, and why?"

She said, "Well, I had an old Chevy that had a good gas gauge on it, but one day it was past empty. I had a bunch of schoolchildren I had to take to school. I told them to all get in the back seat and I would set out for the school, and I wanted them all to pray. The kids were in the back seat praying. We arrived at the school and all the way back home for five days on fumes, but praise the Lord, we made it."

This is a story that is almost impossible to believe. I have a very personal friend who is a very good Christian. He would not say anything that is not the truth. He had a Jeep truck, and I wanted to buy it, but it sold. Now this is what he told me. I have been broke and needed some gas money, and he has had many wonderful things happen in his life that I have known of. The Lord told him to take the garden hose and fill that thing up with water. He told the Lord, "I am a mechanic, and if I fill that up with water, it will mess up everything on my vehicle." The Lord said, "I am telling you to do this." He told the Lord, "Okay, Lord, I will be obey but show you the trouble we are going to have." Therefore, he did as the Lord told him and took the garden hose and filled it up with water. It worked. He just could not believe it. It was a special blessing. He ran on that tank of water for a week, but he never again did that.

I think when we come back after the rapture, we will not have to worry about fuel. I have a friend in California who is developing a new car that will run on air. There are four great big tanks in the bottom of the car. These are air tanks on high pressure so it will make the car run. It is just like the air compressors we have now. This is going to be different and interesting.

Now the flying saucers run on what they call fuel the size of your thumb. They can go thousands of miles. The airplane runs on thousands and thousands of gallons of gas. Flying saucers do not have that; they can go all around the world and into outer space on this special energy. When we come back from the tribulation, I think the Lord will make something like the flying saucers.

Praise the Lord.

Two Separate Occasions

I have read about how Moses' face glowed so very brightly. When I read this passage, I knew this was an incredibly strong type of anointing. The Lord has many different ways to anoint, all of which are fascinating and wondrous, to say the least.

I am going to describe how the Lord Jesus anointed me. Although I was not anointed to the degree Moses was, what a blessing it was to experience such holiness, not once but twice.

The first anointing occurred as I was standing about twenty feet away from the large golden Jesus sign. It was overcast, and I was standing with the sign to my back. I was engaged in conversation with a good friend of mine, just chatting away when my friend exclaimed that my face was suddenly starting to glow, getting brighter and brighter than ever. He asked me if I was all right, as my face was so white and shiny.

The shine started to dissipate, according to my friend, as I obviously could not see it for myself, but was still unusually white. I was told that the color of my face was pure, if that makes any sense. Usually white faces are indicative of illness or heat exhaustion.

The second time I was anointed, I was in a fast food place, of all locations. I won't mention what food chain it was, but I will say that it is a large chain, and everyone has been there, I surely hope. Getting to the point, I was seated in a booth accompanied by two friends, when one exclaimed, "Look at Lee's face. It is getting bright." They asked me if I felt it glowing and I told them, "I do not feel any sensation whatsoever." My two companions were awestruck, having never witnessed such an occurrence.

Since this has occurred twice, I do believe there is significance behind it. I have never heard of anything like this happening or I would have not mentioned this miracle.

I really cannot find any reason as to why this occurred. I will say that people who saw my face glow were stunned, shocked, and astonished. I just will mark this down as another wonder in my personal walk and talk with Lord Jesus, our true healer.

Praise the Lord.

Loss of Healing

Can a person lose their healing? I had better not tell you now, but read on and you will definitely know the answer.

This was at a wonderful revival service at a high school in southern Florida. We had a great service, with so many miracles and healings. After the main service, I laid my hands on a couple thousand folks. Nearly everyone had left. There may have been eighty people left in the lobby. All of a sudden, a car pulled right up to the front, and two girls came out on those aluminum arm braces. They still had to have a person on both sides of them to help them walk, as they were in bad shape. I can remember their legs and bodies looked to be all out of shape; they were immobile.

They said they were sorry to be late, but it was raining very hard. I have to say, it was a very horrific sight. I walked over to one of the girls, both of whom were about twenty-five, and laid my hands on her shoulder and said, "Be healed in the name of Jesus." She fell down like a sack of potatoes and passed out for about two or three minutes. The two people with her had picked her up. Now hear this: she started to jump and dance like a schoolchild.

Then I went to the other young woman. I said to myself, "The Lord cannot heal one and just leave the other one that way." I laid my hand on her and said the same thing, "Be healed in the name of Jesus." Wow the same thing happened; she fell down too. The two friends went over to help her up, but she said, "No, please, I need no help." She jumped right up just like a high school cheerleader, shouting and dancing.

I have told many people who have been healed never to fail to give Lord Jesus praise and worship for all he has done.

Time passed, and unexpectedly, the two young women contacted me. One told me how to get to their place and that she would be waiting for me on the corner. There she was, as she had told me, waving and jumping. I followed her to their home. We went in and sat down on the sofa, and I just could not believe my eyes. The other young woman had those aluminum arm braces leaning on the sofa next to her. Wow, I thought I would never see them again, so right there and then, I knew I had to find the underlying cause of what was going on.

I had to start somewhere, so I started by asking her, "Have you been reading your Bible lately?"

She said, "No, but I guess I should, I suppose."

Wow, I think I am getting somewhere. "Do you pray before you eat anything?"

"No, I really don't, but maybe I should."

Now I am really going to throw the big one out at her. "Do you get down on your knees every night and thank the Lord for that great miracle he did on you?"

Can you believe her next answer? "No, but I probably should."

"You know, if I were you and the Lord did for me what he had done for you, I would be on my knees every night praising him and thanking him for what he did, plus I would be the greatest witness on earth. I would be telling all of your close friends how the Lord gave you such a miracle," I said. I told her to get her nose in the Bible, and to praise Lord Jesus, and before she lets anything touch her lips, to thank him for all she is about to eat and receive. She promised she would, but not with too much enthusiasm.

I prayed and prayed for her with all I had. We said good-bye, and I never heard from them again. I hope she learned a great lesson from this, to remember to thank her Lord Jesus for all he has done.

Never fail to praise and worship your Lord Jesus. Let this be a good lesson for all. Remember this passage:

Everything you do in this whole world will come to pass
But only what you do with Christ will last.

This is one of my favorite sayings about our Lord Jesus.

Praise the Lord.

Wisdom and Knowledge

A beautiful black person came out to see me who was about fifty years old. We sat on the porch, and I was talking with her. She never told me what her problem was, and she did not ask me to pray for her. My chair was close to hers, and as we were talking, my right hand went right over to her heart, so I place my hand on her heart. I said, "Wow, you have trouble with your heart. Your left ventricle is blocked. There is no blood pumping through there."

She looked at me and said, "How in the world did you know? I have been to the doctor. They took many x-rays. This is why I came out here, to see if I could talk with you about it, and you already knew the problem."

I said, "I really do not know why the Lord had me do that, but he did, and he told me what the problem was."

This is what you call the word of knowledge, and the word of knowledge is very powerful. Now that the Lord had given me the word of knowledge, I told her, "You are *healed!*" she looked at me, and all she could do and say was, *"Wow!"* I told her about wisdom and knowledge.

Praise the Lord

Now the word of knowledge is one of the nine gifts of the spirits. One of them is wisdom, and yes, one of them is the word of knowledge. I told her, "If you have wisdom, you have a large beautiful loaf of bread, and if you have knowledge, you own the bakery."

Now this beautiful person came back, and it must have been three weeks later or better. She brought three more of her female friends. Her friends wanted me to pray for them. (We pray for all.) Mrs. So and so went to the hospital, and the doctors said, "What happened? The blood is flowing through there fast."

She told the doctor, "I came out to me the preacher man, and he placed his hand on my heart and said, 'You are healed.'"

The doctor told her, "Yes, you are healed, and the preacher man knew what he was talking about."

Therefore, when her friends knew of what she had done, they too wanted to come and see me to be touched, and prayed for.

I prayed for all three of them, and they were very pleased and happy. It gives me pleasure to see that she came back to allow me to hear and see her wonderful blessing from our creator Lord Jesus.

Thank you, darling Jesus.

Riding My Bike

It was a warm, sunny day, so I decided to ride my bike to the supermarket. I have a large basket on the backside for my groceries. As I entered the parking lot off to my left, I noticed a large black Cadillac. The car had New York plates on it. Two men were getting out and helping a young woman, in I would say her thirties, out of a wheelchair and putting her in the front seat of the car. It looked as though he was actually stuffing her legs in. As I rode past looking at this sight, the Lord told me, "Son, please go back. I want to heal her." I pedaled my bike a little bit farther, and the Lord said it again to make sure I heard him. I turned around and peddled back to the big Cadillac.

By this time, one of the men was putting the wheelchair in the trunk. When approaching a person in this type of situation, you cannot just come on like a gangbuster; therefore, I mentioned my extensive experience with my own mother and sister, who were in wheelchairs. This broke the ice, and I got a nice welcome from the man. I told him I pray for people, and I wondered if it would be okay if I prayed for the young person. He told me she was his wife and to ask her; so far, so good.

We walked around to the front door on the passenger's side, and she lowered the window. The woman had a beautiful smile. Her husband told her that I would like to pray for her if it was all right. With a twinkle in her eye, she said, "Please." I thought to myself at least I was getting somewhere.

I opened the door and asked her how long has it been since she walked. She replied, "Sir it has been over eight years."

I then put my left hand forward and told her to hold my left index finger. She grabbed it with a good solid grip, and for the first time in my life, and as a surprise to me, I said in the name of the "bright morning Star," which is one of Jesus' many names.

To my amazement, she stepped out of that car as if she were born for the first time.

I love using expressions like that; it makes me feel just like a movie star when telling all about the wondrous miracles I've been a part of.

Just as she was starting to get out of the car, I heard the *devil* talk to me in a very loud voice. "You fool; if she falls, you will have a hard time getting her back up." Immediately the Lord Jesus asked me who I thought I was working for. "Son, you work for me, the Lord Jesus." I told the Lord, "Yes, Lord, you are correct. I work only for you."

I held my arm all the way out as she held my finger ever so tightly. We both walked in a very large circle, and every step she took was like her first step. As she and I continued to walk the circle, I would say every time, "In the name of Jesus, how we love thee." The young person gave me a huge hug and a kiss on my neck and could not stop thanking me. I told her, "Remember, Lord Jesus is your healer. I just preach and pray for him. Remember, my dear one."

Thank you, my darling Jesus.

Angels, Angels, Angels

I had some eye surgery done. I had to have my eyes dilated, and during that, I could not see. I have this wonderful, wonderful friend named Victor, and he was so wonderful to come out from his house to the church to take me to the doctor's office, and bless his soul, he would always wait, no matter how long it took. The doctor, is an expert and well known for his eye surgery, which he does on cataracts and other things. In this doctor's office in the waiting area, there is a big-screen TV, and it shows the doctor performing the eye surgery. Victor was so nice, and he took me there at least twenty times or more. When we would leave the doctor, I would always treat Victor to lunch. We would go to a big huge buffet, and the owner there is a wonderful man. On Veterans' Day, he will give all the vets a free meal. The bakery determent and all the food they have are just unbelievable. Victor loves it, and he has to laugh because there is so much food, so his only complaint is he cannot stop eating. One of the last times Victor and I sat down to eat, Victor said to me, "You know, Brother Lee, what I would like to see one time is an angel."

I said, "Victor! Thank you, thank you, if you would have not brought this up, I would have forgot to put this in the Lord's book and mine. Praise the Lord."

Back in Boca Raton, in my ranch home I have a beautiful pool, and all my neighbors loved to come over for a swim and have a party in my back yard. Inside my house, there were two family rooms. One room had a piano, two organs, and a sixty-inch TV. I got done playing the organ one time; I was playing my favorite piece, "When the Saints Come Marching In." I got up from the organ and said, "Lord, you really helped me through that one. I love your anointing. Lord, I love it so much I will take all the anointing you can give me."

Never say that; you can't take all the anointing the Lord can give you. What happened was that there were two angels standing on each side of me, and they picked me up about three feet off the carpet and had my head right next to the ceiling, I was begging them and pleading with them to please put me down. Well, they finally put me down, and they disappeared. "Oh Lord, I apologize to you, and I am so sorry. I will never say that again. I will only ask for a double portion."

When I was standing there, the Lord said to me, "Son, if you took all the anointing, you would be nothing but a little piece of burned toast."

I looked down on the floor and saw a burned piece of toast and said, "Oh no, Lord, not me. I am sorry."

On the front porch of the Jesus Miracle Chapel I built is the next vision of an angel. It was me and lots of Russians, who were friends of mine. One night, they came out. We would pray a lot, and they wanted to learn more of the Bible. About eight of them went inside the church, and when they came back out, they were shaking, and said, "We, we, we, saw an angel." They saw at the far end of the church a great huge white angel, and it was dark out. The angel had lit up the entire back end of the church, which was about ten to twelve feet high.

People on TV say, "Are there really angels?" Yes, it is true, and there are real, live angels out there. If you believe, you will see.

Praise the Lord.

YeeHaw Junction

About thirty-five miles from where I live, there is a little town called YeeHaw Junction. A couple of times a year, we all meet and have a big potluck dinner where everyone brings a special dish of food to pass. After the wonderful meal, we all have a good old-fashioned revival. These people are very close friends of mine, and they have two house trailers. One they live in, and the other is a church.

My good friend who has the potluck is the great-great grandson of Mr. Wigglesworth. Mr. Wigglesworth is well known for his books that are available in all Christian bookstores. It was said that he had raised six to nine people from the dead. He was on my board of directors until he passed away.

After a great service, songs, and music (many different instruments), we would all praise the Lord. Many miracles took place there. It was getting dark out, so like it states in the Bible, we all gave hugs and kisses on the neck, and I parted. While driving home, I was singing to the Lord, and unexpectedly, it came to me. The world's greatest love song ever was sung by a well-know opera singer, Jan Peerce. I used to tell people that I would sing right along with Jan Peerce, and they would say, "As if you know him." I would tell them back in Detroit where I was born, many, many years ago, we had a very large basement where I went down and sang and danced. I would play his record and sing right along with him, so I did tell the truth.

Back to what I was saying; as I was driving home, I remembered the name of the song, but that was it. I said to the Lord, "Well, Lord, I will get the words to that song and sing it to you."

The Lord said to me, "Son, would you like to sing it to me now?"

I said, "I sure would, but I probably have not sung it in at least thirty-five-plus years, Lord."

The Lord told me, "Son, just open your mouth, and I will let the words come out."

I knew the Lord could do anything, anytime, anyway, if it was his will. "It must have been said," I started, and out came all the words. I was so surprised; I cannot even remember thanking the Lord. This is another true miracle. I started to sing the world's greatest love song, and you are probably wondering what it is. It is, "Because of You," and I still sing it to my Lord. I will write it down, and I hope you all enjoy it, do the same, and sing it to our Lord. I know he will bless you all for it. If you like to sing it, sing it with emotions and very slow. Praise the Lord.

Because of You

Because of you, there is a song in my heart.
Because of you, my romance had its start.
Because of you, the sun will shine, the moon and stars will say
You are mine, forever and never to part.
I only live, for your love, and your kiss.
It is paradise to be near you, like this.
Because of you, my life is now worthwhile and I can smile
Because of you.

Can you imagine the Lord putting all those words in my mouth? I could not even remember for all those years. Yes, I really believe he did it, so gladly, because he wanted me to sing this song to him for the rest of my life. I certainly will have the honor and privilege to do so for my Lord.

I really hope you have the same feeling and experience doing it, as I have had for all of my years.

What a remarkable thing for the Lord to do for me.

Thanks again, my darling Lord.

Poem Lady

Down the street around five or six miles lives one of my closest friends, who I have known for about twelve to fourteen years. His name is David, and his wife is named Bonnie. They own a fish market, which is a huge building with lots of coolers, and they sell all types of fish. Some of the fish they sold would go all over the country.

Let me tell you about Bonnie. She writes poems. I have been interested in poems, and I have read most of the best poem books in the world. I have read poems about the sky, water, flowers, trees, and all the beautiful things the Lord has created. Bonnie has written the greatest poems I have ever read. She has several books on the market and is working on her next book to be published. I asked Bonnie, "Does the Lord help you?"

She answered, "Why, Lee, he will tell me to grab a pencil and piece of paper, and he just puts the poems in my head."

She has a new book, which will be coming out soon. Bonnie said to me, "Would you like to hear the last poem I am putting in the book, Lee?" I answered, *"Yes, yes!"* She read it to me, and *wow,* it was the most uplifting, spiritual poem I have ever heard in my life. I told Bonnie, "What I like to do is record your poems on tape, and when I go to sleep or for a drive, I can listen to them." I have let others listen to her poems, and they were just astonished and wanted to know where they could buy her book. Praise the Lord.

Now I would like to tell you of how I met David and Bonnie. They came down as I started building the Jesus Miracle Chapel, and David is a nice man. He said, "You have that miracle sign up, and I sure could use a miracle."

I said, "Well, Jesus is still in the miracle business. What can he do for you?"

David took off his shoe, I do believe it was the left one, and his foot was dark black; about three inches above his ankle was all black. He was going to go back to the doctor in a day, and had no clue what the doctors were going to do and whether it was gangrene, or what. I held his foot. He had just met me and didn't know me from Adam, and I didn't know him from Adam. Therefore, I laid my hand on his foot and prayed that the Lord was going to heal it for him. The very next day, he came down and took off his shoe, and his whole foot was bright pink. Praise the Lord!

Isn't that wonderful? I told him, "Now remember, it was not me. It was the Lord. We both prayed, and the Lord is the one who healed you." After this truly remarkable miracle, we became the best of friends. Every month after that, they gave a donation toward the Jesus Miracle Chapel. David said, "It would be an honor to give you donations to help keep the lights on. If it wasn't for the great big Jesus Miracle Chapel sign, I don't know what would have happened, so it gives me great pleasure to make a donation."

The next time I went down to see them, Bonnie told me that she wanted to call the *Sunday Osceola Paper*. She said, "I wanted to tell them all about you, so they can send out a reporter."

I said, "I could use that."

The phone rang, and it was the reporter, and her name was Linda. We made an appointment, and she came out. What a wonderful person. We sat on the front porch, and I showed her pictures, tapes, and photos of me all over the world preaching. She was so impressed about all of this; she said she was going to make a wonderful article about me. In the Sunday paper, the entire front page was about the Jesus Miracle Chapel, and it had pictures of me, the Lord's last supper, and the gold cross. As I was reading the article, I saw there wasn't enough room for everything on the front page; I was on the back page too. (*Wow!*) She gave me this fabulous write up, and it really did help me. I have a copy of the article with me at all times, and I would like to say that even the president of the United States has never gotten a full page with his picture all over the front, let alone the back page too. I have to laugh that I am the most popular person in the world, and so handsome, that I took up two pages, not just one.

Bonnie's poem book should be coming out soon, and she gave me the last poem to put in my book. I want you all to read this, to see what wonderful miracles the Lord has given Bonnie to write such beautiful poems, out of the Lord's mouth, into Bonnie's mind, and down on paper. This poem is directly from the Lord to Bonnie, and if people would like to get in touch with her, they can let me know, and I will direct them right to her.

Jesus and Me on the Front Porch

It was a beautiful morning, and I was sitting on my front porch, talking to Jesus, when a big red van pulled up. We have a beautiful circle driveway, and you can drive right up to the front of the church doors. Six people got out of the van. Out came a chaplain of the police department, along his two friends and their three wives. I knew the police chaplain very well; he has been a friend of mine for quite some time. They came over and wanted to talk with me. While we were all sitting on the front porch, Jesus was sitting right next to me in the flesh. Jesus leaned over and said, "My son, you know these people cannot see me. I blinded their eyes, but if you tell them to look over at me, I will allow them to see me."

I looked over at the people and told them that Jesus was sitting right next to me in the flesh. I said, "He told me to tell you to look over at him, and you will be able to see Jesus too." Therefore, the people looked over at Jesus where I told them he was sitting, and there they saw Jesus in the flesh. Two of the ladies' hair stood right up on their arms. I could see in their faces that they were astonished. They were taking their hands and trying to rub the hair on their arms to keep it from standing up while saying, "Oh my goodness, we just cannot believe this." They were dumbfounded and speechless. This vision last for around thirty seconds.

The next day, the red van came back, still shaken. They said, "What a wonderful miracle to see Jesus sitting there in the flesh. We just had to come back to tell you. Jesus is so beautiful, and his smile and his teeth. We are just amazed. Amen."

Next, we took the chair that Jesus was sitting in, which is one of those white plastic chairs, and put artificial flowers around the arms of the chair. I bought Jesus flowers just for him. You see, it says in the Bible that Jesus says, "I am the rose of Sharron, the lily of the valley." Therefore, I bought roses and lilies and taped them on the chair. Now when people come to visit Jesus and me, I ask them if they would like to sit in the same chair Jesus sat in. I do not know if there is any anointing left on it, but you can sit in it if you like. All who come say, "Oh yes, please, it would be an honor to sit in the same chair that our brother Jesus sat in."

It was not long after that I was watching TV (an auction), and they were auctioning off a little cigar box that belonged to President Kennedy. I think his cigar box went for approximately $35,000. The next item was his rocking chair. Everyone knows that Kennedy had a bad back and would always sit in his rocking chair. You would not believe what that rocking chair went for; it was for a million and half, just for the rocking chair. I thought, *Wow, could you imagine what the chair Jesus sat in would be worth?*

You hear about the Virgin Mary on the side of a building or waterfall or people say they see just an image of Virgin Mary and busloads of people come just to see her image. Therefore, what I wanted to do is put an article in the paper about Jesus sitting on my front porch in the flesh so thousands of people would come and sit in his chair. Now this was not just a vision; it was Jesus in the flesh. I went to the paper, and no one would write it in their paper, due to some policy. I know that if I could have done this, thousands would have come to see the chair where Jesus sat in the flesh. There would have been no charge to see the chair Jesus sat in.

God bless.

Contribution, Contribution, Contribution

Contribution? I have so many in my mind that will never leave me. I thought this would be a very interesting thing to tell you all about.

The Lord says, "The preacher that feeds you." In other words, he is talking about where you are fed. This is spiritually—a person, church, or ministry that you feed financially. I hope you enjoy this story.

I was sitting on the front porch one day when two big, beautiful cars drove up. I think one was a Towncar and the other a Cadillac. The people got out and were very well dressed and walked up to me. I looked up at them and greeted them, and they said, "We wanted to stop and talk with you."

I said, "Well come in and sit, my children. I am so glad you decided to stop."

I showed them the inside of the church and what I was doing for our Lord. The men stated, "Wow, what an anointed place you have here. We have never seen such a wonderful, anointed place. I can feel the anointing."

Then we all sat down, and I talked with them for over an hour and told them things no other preacher had ever told them. I told them most of the things that I have done and about where I have been. Then I gave them all a picture of Jesus walking on water. After I gave them their blessing and all the information about the Lord, they stood up and said, "You have a nice day now. Bye-bye."

Lee Hoffman

You see, I have a jar on a stand that states, "All donations accepted." Wow, after all of the long talk and blessing I gave them, along with the picture of Jesus walking on water, they gave *not* even a penny or a dollar. I took all that time to bless them. I told the Lord, "It is okay if they did not contribute. I'll preach your name whether they give anything or not."

When you go to church and the collection plate is passed, you put something in. You see, these well-dressed folks, with diamonds and fancy cars, pulled up and got a roadside church service. I gave each one of them an individual service. People all over say, "If you want an individual service, go see the preacher!" I gave them, like I stated, individual service, and they did not thank me or contribute a dime for the Lord.

About forty-five minutes to an hour after these folks left, I was sitting on the porch doing some praying, and this old van drove up with rust on it. The people in the van were in their seventies. They drove up and ask me if they could drive around and see the big glass cross on the side of the building. "*Yes, yes!*" I said. I took them to the side to show them the glass cross. They told me how beautiful it was, and I told them I try to keep the lights on for the world to see. The woman said, "I would be honored to give you an offering."

I said, "Why thank you."

She took the money and kept wadding it up and put it in my hand and said, "This is an offering for the Lord."

"Why thank you, but I never take an offering without praying over it," I said.

I prayed and prayed over the offering and told the Lord to bless them. I told them we would use the offering to the Lord to keep the electric on, so I could keep the lights shining for all to see. I had to unfold it, and as I unfolded it and stretched it out, I saw it was a hundred-dollar bill. Praise the Lord. The man did the same thing. He wadded up a bill and placed it my hand and said, "I want to give an offering too."

I said, "Oh, no, no your wife just gave an offering."

The man said, "Well, that is her offering, and now this is my offering."

I said, "Okay, you get a blessing too." I prayed over it and blessed them. I started to unfold it, and *wow,* it was another hundred-dollar bill. I said to myself, "My goodness sake, here these two wonderful people in an old rusty van, probably just making it on their social security, and each of them gives the Lord a hundred-dollar bill. Not just an hour prior to that, I had people who looked like had the money to offer, with their fancy cars and diamonds, and they gave not a single contribution. You just never know how things will turn out and others' reaction to the Lord with a contribution. Remember, you reap what you sow."

Praise the Lord.

No names will be mentioned in this book; you all know who you are. I would never expose you as they do on national TV.

A Great Anointing

I was over in Taiwan with a group of people. We walked through the town and had a good time there. Then we walked up this little hill on the outskirts of town. There were about eleven or twelve of us. When we reached the top, we stood there looking down on the town, and you could see the town and sidewalks very clearly. We were about a city block away from the town. Out of the clear blue sky, a fellow said, "Why don't you raise your hand and tell them all in the town to fall down?"

I looked at him and said, "Okay." When I waved to all the folks in the town, they all did fall down. I was amazed, and so were the folks who were with me. It looked to me like about one hundred people fell down for a few minutes. This is what you would call being in the spirit.

Allow me to explain this. Many times I have sat on my front porch at the church and have talked and held the hands of at least twenty thousand people who have sat there with me. I held both of their hands and prayed for them. What I cannot believe is that most of the folks I have had the privilege to talk with do not know what the anointing is. You would think in this time and place most of them would know what it meant. I tell them that it is the Holy Ghost putting his spirit on people. He usually uses qualified preachers and anointed to do this.

I watch TV all the time and see preachers on there, and they believe they have a great anointing on themselves. They like to touch folks on their foreheads, and when they do this, the people are supposed to fall backward. Many times this does not happen and it rather belittles the preacher, so he keeps pushing and pushing until they lose their balance so they will fall back. This is not really anointing.

When I stayed in Taiwan and walked through the hotel I was at, the folks who were sitting on the sofas and chairs or standing would fall over as I would walk on by. I was a little amazed, because I did not think the anointing would be that strong on me. This is called being slain in the spirit.

Thank you, Jesus.

Anointed Prayer Cloth

A long time ago in the Bible, Peter and a couple other disciples would go in to town. There would sometimes be someone who knew a sick person who could not get out of bed to go to town, so Peter and the other disciples would give them a handkerchief or apron. Peter would hold the handkerchief up to the Lord and pray on it. All the anointing would go through Peter into the handkerchief or apron for them to lay on the sick so they would get well.

Now I get a little choked up about this story. You see, it was not Peter or the disciples or the handkerchief that would accomplish the healing; it was the anointing the Lord had placed on it. You can take any old handkerchief or apron from anywhere and try this, but it will do no good at all. When Peter preached a sermon of God, he had the anointing, and this is why it worked.

Now people for years have been sending out prayer cloths to folks all over the world, and they wonder why it does not work. It is not the cloth; the person holding the cloth is why it will not work. The person needs to be anointed in order for a miracle to work. You need to have a man of God, or sermon of God, to hold it and pray on it so it will be anointed.

For years I had a roll of red prayer cloth, and I have handed it out for many years. I would take and cut it up and hold each piece in my hand and ask the Lord to anoint each and every one. I had a fellow come not too long ago for a visit. He opened up his wallet and showed me the prayer cloth I had given him seven years earlier. He told me, "I keep it there at all times." I know it has done him a lot of good.

A big, husky guy does not live far from the church. I have seen him at a grocery store; we stopped to chat for a bit. He and his wife told me he had gone to the hospital a day or so before. He told me the doctors told him his stomach was filled with tumors. He had to go back for a biopsy to see if there were benign or cancerous. I had a prayer cloth in my pocket and told him to take it and lay it on his stomach. He went back a few days later to the doctor for his test, and to the his relief, the tumors were all gone. His wife later asked, "Do you think there is still enough anointing left in that little prayer cloth for his eyes?"

I said, "Well, let's see." I took the cloth and laid it on his forehead. He had very thick glasses on; he said his vision became a lot better. He said the main thing he noticed was that when he looks to the left or right out of his eyes, it was a lot better.

What I like to do is to take prayer cloths, pray over them every night to fill them with anointing, and send them out all over the world. If you would like a prayer cloth, I would ask you to send a self-addressed enveloped with a stamp, along with your prayer request. We will take the need and pray over it to anoint it and send it back to you.

Many people have came back and told me how it has worked. We thank the Lord. Prayer requests may be sent to:

Jesus Miracle Chapel
9090 E. U.S. Highway 192
St. Cloud, Florida 34773

May the Lord be with you all.

Chapter 4

Lifting Me out of My Bed in His Arms Telling Me
He Held Lee's Hand over Seven Thousand Times

Blessed Visits

I do not think this experience is going to take very long to tell, but I will try to get in some of the most interesting little details. I am certain that this story is something the world has never heard of.

After the long three-and-a-half-hour service I have with Lord Jesus, we have a little talk, and then I am ready for a good night's sleep.

My darling Lord figured it was not quite time for me to doze off, so he began a ritual that he has been doing for approximately twenty years. Jesus lifts my legs in the air and starts to clap my feet together. Jesus claps them first as if you would clap your hands, around fifteen times, and then stops and drops them. Then this ritual starts all over again. I have had this happen over and over; Jesus sometimes picks me up and flips me on the opposite side of the bed, sometimes a little roughly. I could not even begin to tell you how many times this has happened in the past twenty years. It usually takes place twice a week, and after many years, it has been occurring five times a week, every night.

One night, Jesus picked me up as I counted aloud the number of times: one, two, there, four, five times, yes! It was five times total in a row. Now I am going to tell you something a little harder to believe. One time Jesus picked me up and flipped me on the other side of my bed. I said, "Jesus, you did not find me on that side of the bed, so please why don't you pick me up, and put me back where you found me?"

Can you imagine God's servant telling the man who hung on the cross to put me back where he found me? I would say that you have to be a very good friend to be able to talk to one another like this.

Thank you, my precious Lord Jesus, and do not ever stop!

Praise the Lord.

Apple of My Eye

This is not going to be a very long story, but it was and will always be a highlight in my life, which gives me a little extra boost. Sometimes it helps our faith, which can bring it to a new high.

I was lying in bed just thinking and was very wide awake when, in a heartbeat, Jesus was standing at the foot of my bed. Jesus was right at the right corner of my bed. He was as clear as a bell. Then the Master spoke these words: "Son, you are the apple of my eye."

Then Jesus disappeared as fast has he had appeared. I said nothing. I heard Lord Jesus' words and just took it all in. I thought it was wonderful and thanked Jesus many times in my life.

Time passed, and after a few years, Jesus himself brought up the subject and said, "Son, remember when I called you the apple of my eye?" Jesus wanted to make me feel good by reminding me every so often. I can still hear Jesus say it: "Hey, Lee, you have nothing to worry about. You are the apple of my eye."

Thank you, Lord Jesus. I am sure you cannot buy that, no matter how wealthy you are.

However, little did I know that Jesus would lift me to a higher level than this.

Praise the Lord.

The Many Names of Jesus

As we all know, Jesus has many names he is known by. These are just a few of the most popular ones: Jehovah Nissi (the Lord is my banner), Jehovah Rafah (God our healer), Jehovah Shalom (Lord our peace), and Jehovah Jireh (the Lord will provide). It also tells in the Bible that he is the "Rose of Sharon, and the Lily of the Valleys." There is one name I like the best of them all, the Bright and Morning Star. I have just used that name of his, and when I do, I see the most wonderful miracles happen. Lord, you are my bright morning star.

When I first started this ministry of healing, I heard the name Jehovah Rafah, which means God our healer. I was young and did not know too much about it, but people said if you use that name, Jehovah Rafah, people would be healed. Therefore, when I heard that, I thought all you had to do is go around and touch people and say, "Jehovah Rafah" and they would be healed. The Lord must have thought I had a lot of faith in that word. I have touched people who had backaches, who were sick, and who were dying of anything you can image. I touched them and said, "Jehovah Rafah heals you," and I would repeat it. I believed that was all I had to say. The Lord must have said, "Here this young man saying and touching all those people, and saying Jehovah Rafah." They all would be healed. I remember one time on a golf course, there was a man who had a bad back, and we were trying to get him back in the golf cart so he could get back to the clubhouse. The man's back was in such pain, so I got out of the golf cart to talk with him.

I asked the man, "Do you believe in Jesus?"

He replied, "Oh yes, I am a good Christian."

I looked at him and said, "Well, Jehovah Rafah heals you." Then I touched him. The man jumped right out of the golf cart and said, "I feel so good. I can play another nine holes."

Praise the Lord.

Interpretation of Tongues

In the Bible, there are nine gifts of the spirit. The nine gifts are as follows:

- The gift of wisdom
- The gift of knowledge
- The gift of discernment
- The gift of faith
- The gift of healing
- The gift of working of miracles
- The gift of prophecy
- The gift of tongues
- The gift of the interpretation of tongues

I knew a long time ago one of the largest churches there ever was did not believe in speaking in tongues. They believed it was of the devil. I wondered how God could say in his Bible that he is going to give you a beautiful gift of the spirit and you could think it is of the devil. This big church thought it to be the devil, and I will not say which one, but how in the world could they even say or think that? Now, after all these years, this church finally believes in speaking in tongues. The Lord must have opened their eyes. I just cannot imagine thinking this if God comes to you and says, "I have a special gift of the spirit."

One of the greatest preachers who ever lived just passed away recently. He went to the church, and he was speaking in tongues and laid hands on a person who was healed. This is a famous story. They kicked him out of the church just because he spoke in tongues.

I was sitting on my sofa in my beautiful home, and Jesus was sitting on my left side. He took my left hand and held it, and said, "Son, that language you have been speaking is very nice, but I am going to take it away from you now. I am going to give you a special language for you to speak, and only you and I will understand." The Lord squeezed my hand very tight and said, "Now here is the language for you to speak to me." I tried to remember the other language, and I just could not. It was so very nice of him to hold my hand and speak a special language between the Lord and his son Lee.

Dropped Blood Pressure

Whenever I find myself in a supermarket or drug store equipped with a blood pressure machine. I sit down and run the test, which always enumerates a display of perfect, ideal results. Despite this fact, however, my blood pressure was not always so good. After watching my blood pressure creep higher and higher, my growing fear prompted me to entertain the thought of asking the Lord for assistance in lowering the numbers. I then thought that I would not ask the Lord for his assistance, since he has given me numerous miracles already. I did not have the heart to ask for another favor of him again.

After a few weeks, I decided to go take a test, and to my dismay, my blood pressure was at an all-time high. Out of fear, I tested again twice more and found the same results. That was the moment I made the decision to get down on my knees that evening to ask the Lord to lower my blood pressure.

That night, I got down on my knees and prayed, "Lord Jesus, I hate to ask, but could you please lower my blood pressure? It is very high, and I would greatly appreciate it if you would do this favor for me."

As it were, the next morning I took out my at-home blood pressure testing kit and started a concise and careful test to procure an accurate reading. What was on that screen was hard to believe; my blood pressure had actually dropped over one hundred points in a single evening. I tested repeatedly, just to make sure there were no mistakes. The next thing I did was tell Lord Jesus how thankful and appreciative I was for his timely and gracious assistance with my blood pressure, dropping it so much and so fast. I called Jesus, "My darling" fifty times that day, and told him he sure did a fabulous job on my blood pressure. I said, "Lord, you sure did a fabulous job. I bet you did it last night when I was on my knees asking for your help."

Jesus said in a very loud and clear voice, *"No, Son."* Then I questioned if he did this deed during the night while I was asleep. Again he said in a loud, clear voice, "No, Son." I am not the kind of man who can let something so wondrous go without an answer; curiosity always gets the best of me. Therefore, I had to ask Jesus, "When, Lord, did you do this for me?" Lord Jesus replied in such a sweet voice that he helped me before I even asked him for the help, but at the same time I decided to turn it over to Jesus.

I have to relate that when I wrote about this holy anecdote, tears were flowing from my eyes and down my cheeks like never before. I could not even write these words without wiping away the tears. The love the Lord Jesus has for us is something so beautiful that I cannot even verbalize it. Words simply would not do Lord Jesus' love for us justice.

It was fourteen years ago when I had this problem with my blood pressure. Whenever I visit a store and see the blood pressure machine, I remember the wonderful miracle Lord Jesus did for me.

Praise the Lord.

New Teeth

This incredible experience is going to involve every person on earth, because everyone has had teeth at one time, and many now have dentures. This all happened at a large revival meeting in Kissimmee, Florida, at the famous Tupperware Auditorium. Another preacher and I were there for six days, during which we witnessed all kinds of miracles, including the blind seeing for the first time in their lives.

What I am going to describe in detail is an occurrence that to date remains unheard of by whomever I tell, so I am almost certain you have never heard of this happening before. Here goes. The two preachers involved, one of whom is me, called someone out of the audience, and the person would leave his or her seat and go stand out in the aisle. We would stand about two feet in front of the person and ask what he or she needed or wanted or would we tell him or her what the Lord told us was wrong with him or her.

The Holy Bible states in the book of Corinthians that one of the nine gifts of the spirit is called the word of knowledge. In this particular case, I asked a man to come and stand in the aisle and tell me what he needed. This man, not bashful in nature at all, exclaimed that he needed a new set of teeth. He proceeded to turn to the audience of about two thousand five hundred people and visually demonstrate with his index finger the abhorrent condition of his mouth. His lower teeth had suffered from tooth decay and were brown and rotten; his upper teeth were a sight. There were rotten teeth on one side and a long, gnarled single one on the other side, reminiscent of a fang. I was less than two feet away from this man, and I seemed to have a direct view into his mouth. What a terrible sight! I cannot ever recall seeing a mouth quite so horrific! I thought the man had a great request for the Lord in asking for new teeth, and I laid my hands on his shoulder and said, "Jesus, give him new teeth." I thought this request was for a big miracle. I have to say that I have seen some big miracles in the past that left me surprised and astonished, but I really was not ready for what I was going to witness happen in a twinkle of an eye.

The man's mouth was closed, and I told him to open his mouth. I figured that his mouth must have been closed for three to five seconds. He opened his mouth in the very same manner in which he initially revealed it, with an index finger on either side, stretching his lips as wide as possible. What did I see? It was a true miracle. Lord Jesus, the wonders you do will never cease.

Thank you, my darling Jesus.

Spirits, Spirits, Spirits

This is a very interesting subject, and that is why Jesus and I have been personally discussing the subject for at least fifty years. I will try to tell you the truth, just as Jesus has told me so many times, and he has quoted me so many Scriptures in the Bible about them, the same Scriptures I have read about for over fifty years, so I know all the verses. He reminds me of memorization for all these fifty years. Jesus says the truth will set you free. He wrote it, and I will just quote it.

I will start talking about the spirits with God's help. First, we must know that there are just two spirits and only two. One is the good spirit, and the other one is the evil spirit. That is the good and the bad. Let us name the two different ones and tell our readers where they come from.

The good spirit is the true spirit of Father God called the Holy Spirit. He is the spirit the Bible says Father God sent. God sent his Holy Spirit to take Jesus out of his grave and set him on the right side of his Father God. Therefore, who is the other spirit that is the bad spirit? You guessed it. It has to be the devil and his demons. Another name in the Bible refers to him as Satan. I hope you now understand who the two spirits are. If you did not know that exactly, you see how much smarter, or should we say intelligent, you are.

In the Bible, the Lord has a special name for everyone who works with spirits that are not the Holy Spirit of Father God. This is what God refers to them in his holy work called the holy Bible as "revilers," such as fortune-tellers, palm readers, and many others in this nature. These are not from his Holy Spirit, so they naturally have to be from the other spirit. Remember, there are only two, so if there are not from Holy Father God, they have to be from the devil and his demons. Yes, it is very nice to hear someone else say, "I see your grandmother or sister, or brother, or someone else. They say they had a good time with you; they are thinking about you now and are always looking over your shoulder hoping to be with you someday." Yes, you have heard this and similar sayings on many different talk shows on television. Yes, it gets people excited, and some of them believe this baloney, or should I say a big lie from Satan. Have you ever heard someone say on television, "I talk to Jesus and the Holy Spirit of God, and he told me to tell you this"? No, never in all my life have I ever heard it from all those revilers.

I am going to get into it a little deeper, so I will have to start quoting some of God's Scriptures from his Holy Bible. If I just quote it and tell you it is in the Bible, you might not believe me. If I told you where to find it in the Holy Bible, you would probably just keep reading and never look it up, so I am going to take the time for your sake. I will not only to tell you what book it is in the Holy Bible, but I will also write down the chapter and verse reference.

In my lifetime, I have maybe cast out a thousand demons. Who gives the devil the power to do all of this? I am going to tell you by quoting the scripture. Just let me explain that the power of Satan is nothing to the power I am going to explain. Do you know that when you sang that song, "Twinkle, Twinkle Little Star," it has been proven by huge telescopes, like the Hubble telescope, that those little tiny stars are not so little at all? Most of them are thirty times larger than the planet earth, but they are so many light years away in space that they just look small.

Okay, now take a seat for this one. The devil in the last days, which we are in now, will pull the stars right out of the sky or space. Yes, that is just what he is going to do. It is much more than telling you your grandmother said to tell you hello. The next unbelievable miracle the devil will do is that he will tell the rivers and your drinking water to turn to blood, not just regular blood, but dead blood. I guess it is about time I tell you who is going to give him this power. You probably never would have guessed it: it is our Holy Father God. I am not only going to tell you right now why God gave him this power, but I am also going to write that book so you can understand.

All through the book of Revelation, many times, the Lord is talking and says," I gave power to the devil to do this, and to do that." I have read the book of Revelation at least one hundred times forward and one hundred times backward, and then memorized a good portion of it, which I thought was most interesting.

Why does God give the devil this power? He explains very carefully in the book of Revelation that he, God, gives the devil power to deceive those who dwell on the earth.

In Revelation 13:13–14, it states Satan does great wonders that make fire come down from heaven to the earth in the sight of men (chapter 14). He deceives them, and the Lord gives him the power to deceive them and make them believe a lie. It is like this: the devil and the Lord both want your mind, but the devil is much pushier. It says in the Holy Bible that the devil comes to lie and to kill and destroy. I really hate to give him any credit at all, but we have to face the facts: he is doing a fabulous job. He is in the father of lies, and he sure is doing a great job of killing. Just turn your television on and watch the evening news, see what the main subject is. The devil is worse then any storm. He loves to play mind games on all to destroy as many as he can.

The Lord says if you do not turn your mind over to him, he will give your mind to the devil, and the devil will own you. You will not own yourself and Father God will not own you. The Lord says, "I will come to give you life and more abundantly" and he lets you choose, so let us choose the right spirit." This is your creator, the one who gave us our nose and toes, and he died on the cross for all of our sins.

Read what the Lord has to say in 2 Thessalonians 2:8–12.

Praise the Lord.

Devil in My Bed

After a long and wonderful prayer evening with Bible reading about the Last Supper and ending up at about 3:30 AM, I got in bed and started to say the last of my prayers. That's when it happened. The devil jumped on me and took the large pink bedspread cover and wrapped it around my neck about two or three times. It felt as if it weighed two hundred pounds or more. I said, "Devil, I am going to teach you a good lesson." I always keep a .38-special under my pillow fully loaded with special shells, and as I started to reach under my pillow, I was completely frozen. I could not move my arm at all.

The devil was choking me and getting the best of me, and my breath was being shut off. Wow, what a terrible situation to be in. I finally yelled out to Jesus, and when I finally got his name out of my mouth, *"Jesus,"* the devil flew off me and hit the wall about eight feet from the bed with a loud bang! I unwrapped my pink bedspread from my neck and was sort of put out. I said, "Jesus, I thought I was you, boy, and you let that old devil do that to me. The devil could have killed me, Jesus."

Jesus said, "Son I just wanted you to know the power in my name."

I said, "Well, you have made your point, so please, we don't have to use the devil as an example anymore."

They say that every demon in *hell* trembles at the sound of the holy name of Jesus. Experiences like that make me realize Jesus will go to any length to not only prove his point but also desires to teach us very important ways to protect us from our enemy, Satan himself.

Thank you, my darling Jesus, for that great lesson.

Praise the Lord.

Jesus' Favorite Song

Do you know Jesus' favorite song? Yes, there are many songs Jesus loves, but has he ever sat down and held your hand? Well, I have had the privilege of Jesus holding my hand and telling me his favorite song. I do know his favorite song.

When I take a bath, I love to sit down with a brush with a pearl handle, which my mother bought about sixty years ago. It is still to this day like new. While in the bathtub, I love to sing holy songs and church songs that give the Lord all the honor. Jesus walked right up to my bathtub and said, "Son, I want you to sing my favorite song." Wow, I was getting close now to having the pleasure to know his favorite song. I said, "Why sure, Jesus. What's your favorite song?" Jesus leaned over and said, "Holy, Holy, Holy." *Wow!* I knew that song from way back. It's a very popular song. I'd like to tell you know how it goes.

> Holy, holy, holy! All the saints adore Thee,
> Casting down their golden crowns around the glassy sea;
> Cherubim and seraphim falling down before Thee,
> Who was, and is, and evermore shall be.

> Holy, holy, holy! Though the darkness hide Thee,
> Though the eye of sinful man Thy glory may not see;
> Only Thou art holy; there is none beside Thee,
> Perfect in power, in love, and purity.

Holy, holy, holy! Lord God Almighty!
All Thy works shall praise Thy Name, in earth, and sky, and sea;
Holy, holy, holy; merciful and mighty!
God in three Persons blessed Trinity!

As soon as the Lord told me that this was his favorite song, I started to sing it about fifty times a day. I thought, *Wow with all the great music preformed and all the rock stars, I am so privileged to have the Lord tell me his favorite song.* A lot of you have sung this song, and now it gives me great honor to allow all of you to know the Lord's personal favorite song. I just have to tell you all this. There was this adorable little girl, and I was talking with her parents and telling them the Lord's most favorite song. This little girl looked up at me and said, "I know Jesus' favorite song." I said, "Really? What is it, my dear?" She sang it to me:

Jesus loves me, this I know
For the Bible tells me so

Was not that just so sweet? This little girl learned that song and thought it was Jesus' favorite song.

Lord, we love you, and we glorify your name. Thank you for allowing us to personally know the Lord's favorite song.

The Lord reminded me of another one of his songs. I will praise the Lord at all times. All times his praise shall remain constantly in my mouth. One time I was in the bathroom sitting on the commode and talking with the Lord after the hurricane. I was down in the valley talking with the Lord and said, "Lord, why do not you take me right now? I spent all of my time and hours, building the Jesus Miracle Chapel, and in a day it was blown down by a hurricane." I was so down in the dumps, I told the Lord to just please take me now.

The Lord said, "Son, if you would like your own private rapture, I shall give it to you know."

"Wow, Lord, you would do that for me? Well, can I think about this?" After thinking about it, I told the Lord, "Lord, it would be very selfish of me to tell you, 'Yes, take me now. Give me my own private rapture,' after you have shown me personally what my home will look like in heaven and all the great wonders you and I have done. I cannot be a chicken and look for the easy way out. So my apologies to you, Lord. I want to work for you, and I know I can do my good work for you down here. I want to go to heaven and take as many of your children with me as I can."

Praise the Lord.

Chapter 5

Raising the Dead

China River
Largest Restaurant

Life

Raise the dead? Yes, I am proud and privileged to have my Lord Jesus decide to use me, his servant, to perform such a wonderful miracle. I will, in complete detail, tell you where and how it happened.

Another preacher and I were in the Tampa Theater, in Tampa, Florida. We had a revival there for about a week. I want to mention his name, as I rarely do, but I worked with him for such a long time, and took many glorious trips to the Holy Land in Israel with him. I learned more from him than all the preachers combined. His name is W. V. Grant Jr. after his father, which I never had the privilege of meeting. I understand he was also respected as a great man of God before he passed away.

Around the second day of the revival at the theater, he was preaching, and I was sitting on a chair close to him on the stage near the altar. All at once, I saw a man fall over about four rows from the rear. I quickly jumped up and ran down the center aisle.

The man was a large man, over 250 pounds. He was on the floor between a few of the chairs. I had about three people help me pick him up, and that was a real big job—like two sacks of potatoes.

We all carried him out to the lobby and laid him on the red carpet on the floor. I started to pray for him, and in no time at all, the wonderful fire rescue squad came in and told me quickly to get my hands off from him because they were going to use the thumpers on him, and I would be electrocuted. They tried their best, with no luck. They also had a very large needle and syringe they put into his heart, as I understood, and stood by to watch. After a long time with no response, the firefighters said to me, "He is as dead as he is ever going to be, so if you want to pray for him, please do so now."

Now by that time, there were about forty or so more people standing around looking at this scenario.

The Lord then clearly said to me, "Son, lie right on top of him and speak life into him." I did not mind laying my hands on him and praying for him, but I looked around and saw at least forty-plus people watching, with me on my knees praying for him. *Okay,* I thought to myself, *that is not too bad,* and I always do as the Lord tells me to do. I said a prayer and lay on top of the dead man in front of all the folks watching. It took a little nerves or guts. I prefer the word *guts,* but I am obedient to what the Lord says.

The man naturally was on his back, and I got off my knees and lay right on top of him, his belly on my belly. I kept telling him that Jesus was going to make him live. About the third or fourth time I said that, he came right out of it and lived.

Thank you, Lord Jesus. I was there and did what you told me to do, or I think he would have been lost forever. As it was, the fire department took him to the hospital to have him checked out.

The next evening, his wife came to me during the revival. She was so grateful for what I, or I should say the Lord Jesus, had done. She told me that her husband was feeling very well, and she thanked me again. The look in her eyes and the thanks she gave me were better than any donations I have never taken, but her holding my hand with all the gratitude she exuded will always be in my memory.

Thank you, my darling Lord Jesus, for trusting in me once again.

Praise the Lord.

Casting out the Demons

Yes, casting out demons is a very interesting, but more than that, a very important subject. The Lord Jesus and I have discussed the subject so many times, and he definitely told me he wanted me to put this in the book.

He knows very few people really know much about it, and some do not even believe it, let alone know that they have talked to many people who have loads of demons in them. My personal walk and talk with Jesus has given me the opportunity to cast out hundreds, maybe thousands, or more demons. Through the following stories, I will try to educate you in full about how they live in you, and some people will claim you are definitely wrong or insulting until they actually hear them talking inside of themselves. They are being told to come out. I will begin with my neighbor who lives just two doors next to me in a pristine town of Florida.

To prepare you for this, I will call my neighbor Joe. I was passing out some beautiful white Bibles trimmed in gold to my neighborhood and told them they could have as many as they needed or wanted at no charge. Now this Joe was the nicest, kindest helper in the neighborhood. He would cut the grass or trim trees for anyone who needed help. Joe helped me trim about thirty trees around my beautiful pool home. In one word, Joe is what you would say one of the perfect neighbors; he would greet everyone with a happy smile. He was just a happy-go-lucky person.

I was passing out these beautiful holy Bibles, and saw Joe, who was out in his lawn. I approached him and said, "Hi, Joe, I have been giving these nice Bibles out to the neighbors. Would you like one? They are free. You may have as many as you like."

Joe looked up at me and replied, "You know where you can shove those Bibles. Don't try and bring that crap over here." As he belittled the holy Lord's Word, I could see the demons dancing in both of Joe's eyes. In a nice way, I told Joe not to take that attitude, knowing we were going to be living just a door away.

It was not too long after Joe died that his wife came over to my house and asked me to come over to her home because she would like to have a talk with me. She had a lot to show me. She had slept in one room, and Joe had a room of his own. She told me the demons in his room kept her awake all night, and she had to keep screaming at them all night long.

We went into Joe's room, and she showed me that all the drawers in the highboy dresser, about six or more, were pulled out and emptied all over the floor. He had beautiful clothes in the closet, and they were all thrown on the floor. She then took me out to the kitchen, and on the round glass table, she showed me about five or six bottles of pills he was on. Joe's wife relayed that the demons would take all the bottles of pills and toss them all over the kitchen floor and she then had to pick them up and try to put them in the right bottle. I asked her how long it had been going on, and she told me since Joe had died, about four months ago.

I told her I had seen the demons in Joe's eyes, remembering that day in the yard, but when Joe died, the demons would have certainly gotten out in a hurry; they do not stay in a dead person. She described how it was driving her crazy, and she wanted me to help her get the demons to move out. I told her I would be glad to and not to be surprised if I raised my voice, as sometimes I love to shout at demons.

People all come for help from a man they know is a real, dedicated man of God, not the bartender where they spend most of their money. In this case, I want to make it perfectly clear, neither one of them visited bars, in respect of them both.

Demons be gone.

Praise the Lord

Chapter 6

Sound Asleep

Through the Woods

I believe this story is bound to be one of the most intriguing, driving experiences anyone has ever heard or read.

I was driving my car, a late-model Cadillac, on a trip starting in Florida and destined for Michigan. My driving companion was a close female friend who I had actually dated for about five years during the time I knew her. My companion's mother resided in Michigan, and she was going to visit her mother, and I was closing a financial matter for the sale of my Michigan home. This trip to Michigan commenced with an 11:00 AM exit. We proceeded north on pleasant, sunny, peaceful roads, devoid of traffic. Our trip seemed to have a perfect start.

If you would, imagine traveling in this Cadillac at a speed of sixty-five miles per hour with the windows up and the air conditioning. It seems trivial in regard to speed or driving fast. I glanced over at Gloria, my traveling companion, to find her sound asleep. Making light of the adage sleeping like a baby, I was glad that Gloria was napping. I knew that the arduous and lengthy trip ahead of us would require us to take turns driving.

After several hours, I found myself quite sleepy as well. Gloria was still asleep in the passenger seat. I do not believe it was very much longer before I was also sound asleep, blanketed in a deep, trance-like sleep, not capable of driving. Obviously, someone else had assumed the responsibility of driving the car.

The car ventured off the road into thick, tree-filled woods, where concise navigation was necessary to avoid hitting the trees that were spaced in close proximity to each other. We were headed for a steep drop, approximately one hundred feet, which, without divine intervention, would have been the end for Gloria and me.

The tracks made a sharp turn to the left. Just as the car was headed over the drop, it headed back to the main highway, as if it were on autopilot, and drove over the smooth concrete of the main highway, coming up to the pavement. Both front wheels hit the surface at the same time, shaking and bouncing the car, which resulted in a broken set of shock absorbers.

We were fortunate that no cars were coming from either direction as the car came to a stop. We evaluated the situation at hand, caught our breath, and praised Lord Jesus for seeing us through the wildest wakeup call, which I would never wish to re-experience, nor would want anyone else to experience. We got out to witness what had just happened by seeing the tracks and the path we had taken. We were amazed that we were still alive. Praise our darling Jesus.

We proceeded on our voyage with the two front shock absorbers completely broken. Gloria and I, needless to say, had to take the Cadillac in for some much-needed repairs. While the car was on the hoist, the two mechanics commented to me that they had never seen a car that had two broken shock absorbers resulting from a single incident. When I told the two men about what Gloria and I had just experienced, they verbalized, "Someone up there was really looking down on you." It made my day just to hear their insights and the meaning of the words, agreeing that I was indeed blessed.

This friend is the great power of our sweet Lord Jesus.

Praise the Lord.

Rainbow

On my way back from a very successful revival, I was driving back to my home in Boca Raton, Florida, in my large Pace Arrow motor home. I like it because it was all self-contained, and I could stop and pull in a large parking lot, take a nice shower, and go to sleep after a little bite to eat.

I was on a long strip of highway, and as I was looking ahead, I saw the most beautiful and vivid-colored rainbow in a very large half circle way in front of me. I was talking to the Lord Jesus about how beautiful it was and how bright the colors were. The Lord then took it out of the sky in front of me and laid it down in front of me on the highway about five to eight miles in front of me. It then started to come down the highway toward me and got closer all the time. Now it was about ten feet in front of me. Now I was driving on top of it, and it was even coming into the motor home. I was sitting up high with a huge window to look out. I had a floating feeling as I was riding on the rainbow about eight feet about the cement pavement. I was alone on the highway; there were no cars behind me and none coming toward me.

Maybe the Lord had something to do with that beautiful rainbow that went on for at least eight miles. I should say I was floating on the top of it because that is the way it felt, but it did not seem like it was going very fast. It was sort of a slow, soft ride. I have heard many people say for years, "How would you like to ride on a rainbow?" It's quite a saying. Well, I can now say yes, I would like to ride on a rainbow again, because it was a big thrill in my life gliding on the top of it for those glorious eight miles.

I might mention, if you have not read about it in the Bible, the Lord Jesus states that the reason he developed the rainbow and put it in the sky was to let people seeing it be reminded Jesus will never use a flood to cover the earth again. Yes, it is in the Bible, just as I said. I look in the sky all the time hoping to ride the rainbow once again.

Praise the Lord.

Chapter 7

The Ark Covenant

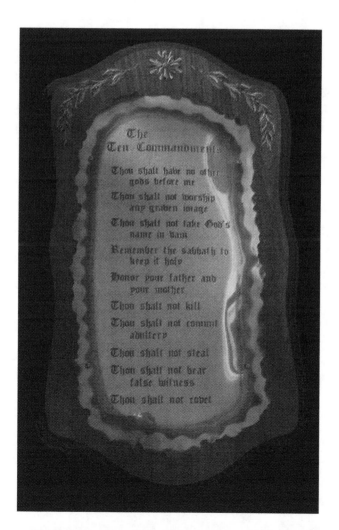

Weight on my Shoulders

I was lying in bed in my trailer. The lights were out, and I was saying my prayers. Then, out of nowhere, a light came into my room. I looked around to see what it was, and it was Lord Jesus standing there with the ark of the covenant on his shoulders. The ark of the covenant has two poles coming out of each end. There have to be two people on each end to carry the ark on their shoulders.

When Lord Jesus appeared in my bedroom, he alone was carrying the ark of the covenant on his shoulders, and there was no one on the other end. I looked to see who else was helping Jesus carry it, and there was no one else. Lord Jesus does not need anyone to help him carry the ark; he alone can do it with all his glory and power. Lord Jesus came over to my bedside and asked me, Brother Lee, if I would carry the ark of the covenant for him the rest of the night. Imagine Lord Jesus asking me to carry the ark of the covenant for him the rest of the night; what an honor. I told Lord Jesus, "Why yes, just put it on my shoulders." I carried the ark on my shoulders for a very long time, and I tell you, it was getting very heavy. I finally went to sleep thanking Lord Jesus for giving me the honor and pleasure to accept such a wonderful gift from our creator.

Now many people have said that the ark of the covenant is the most holy thing in the world. Different countries have claimed it, and I hear on TV that they talk about the ark and claim to not know where it is. Many preachers and others believe that Lord Jesus has it with him up in heaven with him.

When Lord Jesus does wonderful things for me like this, he always comes back to me a couple of days later. I was sitting up by the church on my porch, and Lord Jesus came to me and said, "Son, do you remember when I had you carry the ark covenant for me?"

I answered, "Why yes, Lord, and it was heavy, but it was just an honor for you to ask me." You see, Lord Jesus will always come back to me in a few days to verify all the great and glorious things he has done for me.

Lord Jesus said to me, word for word, "Son, do you know what it represented?"

I said, "Sure, Lord." I told him about the Ten Commandments and what it meant, and Lord Jesus replied, "Son, I will tell you what it represented in your case. It represented you selling everything you have—selling your home in Boca Raton, sailboats, cars, yachts, giving it all away, and coming here to build me the Jesus Miracle Chapel all by yourself so people all over the world can come here to be healed."

I did not intend to write a book at all at that time. All I wanted to do was build the church. I asked Lord Jesus, "Well, what I should name the church?"

Lord Jesus said, "Why, Son, the Jesus Miracle Chapel."

I said, "Sounds good to me, Lord." I did just as Lord Jesus asked me to.

This is how Lord Jesus reminded me of him having me carry the ark of the covenant for him on that glorious night.

Every time I watch television and people talk about the ark, I have to chuckle and look to Lord Jesus and say, "Why, I know where it is. One night I had carried the ark for our wonderful, darling creator, Lord Jesus."

Praise the Lord.

Thank you, my darling Jesus

Altar Piece

The Lord reminded me about this little story, and I have to tell you all about it.

When Nagasaki, Japan, was bombed and leveled off, the Japanese came to me, Brother Lee, and told me that they were going to build a Christian church in Nagasaki, Japan, and they had heard that I build altar pieces. They wanted to know if I would design them some nice altar pieces and candelabras and build them all by hand, and send them off to Japan.

I had a company called, "Altar Pieces by Hoffman." I did many churches in Detroit and different cities and in some of the nicer neighborhoods. I did all the beautiful wrought iron around their homes and inside their homes and on their balconies for probably thirty years. I was well known in Detroit because of Altar Pieces by Hoffman. They got a hold of me and asked me if I would do the altar pieces for them and get them to Japan for their opening services. I did get them done, and I worked very hard on them. They came out very nice, and I got them to them two weeks before services. I have some pictures of some of the candelabras and altar pieces. The organization that was responsible for all of this and paid for everything was a large Methodist Church. I want to thank them for paying for this to be done for them to have these pieces in time for their services. It gave me great honor and pleasure to build these all by hand for our friends in Japan.

Altar Pieces
Designed by Hoffman

Jordan River

I have been in Jerusalem so many times, it is the most wonderful place to visit and see. The Jordan River is in Israel, and across from it is where our creator was baptized, which is called Bethany. It also states that Jesus was baptized in the Jordan River by John the Baptist.

The photo above shows where I and another preacher would baptize people in the Jordan River. There is a rail where people get in line to be baptized. They would get into the river, and we would hold their nose, and then place their head into the water and say, "We baptize you in the name of the Father, the Son, and the Holy Ghost." They really like that, and in the Bible, it says that you come out of the water, which is the true way of being baptized. Baptism is coming out of the water, not when you sprinkle a little water on a baby's forehead in a church. This is what you call a dedication, because you don't want to take a little baby and submerge it in the water. You wait for the child to be older, and then you may submerge him or her in the water.

As I have said, I have been to the Jordan River many, many times to do baptisms. People would come by the busloads to accept the Lord their creator into their lives. I have had my share of baptizing people.

Now in the back of the church I have built for Lord Jesus, I have a pond so when people want to come here for prayer and healing, and for someone to listen, they may be baptized if they like. I have baptized many back there.

I remember one night around ten o'clock someone knocked at the door. It was my friend Peter, who is from Russia, and he had five of his friends with him. Peter had told me that he and his friends are true believers of the creator and that they were getting ready to travel back to Russia. They had a favor to ask of me. Peter told his friends about me, the preacher man, and suggested they come out to me to be baptized. In the middle of the night, I took a flashlight out with me, some of them put on their swimsuits, and we walked over to the pond and got into the water. I had the honor and privilege to baptize them all. They were all so happy that they were going back to Russia baptize. Others who come out who have asked to be baptized say to me, "Just do not sprinkle water on me. We wish to be submerged into the water." I cannot tell you how many people over the years I have baptized.

I would like to take the time to thank all of you who chose to be baptized by me, the preacher man, and to take your creator, Lord, Jesus into your heart.

May the Lord be with thee.

W. V. Grant

Rev. Lee Hoffman
W. V. Grant Jr.
Amp. Theater Caesarea
Jerusalem

I think that it is only proper and very respectful of me to mention some of the preachers whose crusades and revivals I have attended. Most of these I have actually taken part in with them. I have always been actively involved. I would like to mention some of them. I have learned so much from different ones of them. Out of all of some preachers, the one I was closest to is Mr. W. V. Grant. I had the honor of being his assistant.

Everywhere Mr. Grant has been or went, all the preachers have remarked on his wonderful gifts he has carried with him. Mr. Grant talented is, and it gives me great joy and pleasure to mention it, the word of knowledge. I would rush into a service with Mr. Grant, and we would start it together. I have to chuckle, because Mr. Grant would know the people's name, phone number, address, birthday, and personal things of that nature. I would get a big kick out of how he knew all these things. Mr. Grant would say, "I see a Mr. So and So," and a woman would reply, "Why that is my doctor."

I remember one time we got a woman out of the audience, and we had her stand in the aisle. I was in front of her, and Mr. Grant was behind her. Mr. Grant would say, "Mrs. So and So" and he did not know her name at all. Then he would tell her everything in her entire body that was going wrong. Mr. Grant told her, "You have cancer of the liver, and you have cancer here and there."

She would say back to him, "How—how did you know that?"

He would tell her, "The Lord told me your problems, and now you are completely healed. You can go to the doctor and you come back. I will be here all week, so you can let us all know the power of our wonderful creator Lord Jesus that you have been healed."

Mr. Grant started talking about someone with a certain condition, and he would look all the way back to the rear of the theater and saw a woman in a white shirt, and he would ask her to stand up. Mr. Grant said, "Is your name so and so, and is your doctor so and so?"

She said, "Why," with hesitation in her voice, "yes it is, sir."

I'm getting a little choked up telling you this. Mr. Grant said to her, "Why, ma'am, you have the same trouble as the other lady, don't you?"

"Why yes I do," she answered.

"Ma'am, while the Lord was healing her, you yourself were praying for your own pain and troubles. The Lord has healed you also. You may sit down and go to your doctor to see that you have been healed too."

I have learned so much from W. V. Grant, about the word of knowledge that I myself have used it on several occasions.

After many of the revivals we went to, we would never just walk off the stage and leave. No, the people who came would form a very long line, and Mr. Grant and I would go up to each one and touch them all. There had to be at least fifteen hundred in my line and fifteen hundred in Mr. Grant's line. We would lay our hands on every single one and pray for them all. We had four or five catchers with us, and the reason for that is sometimes people would fall down from the anointing before we could even touch them. There were so many people piled up like a cord of wood, but as I said, we would stay right there till the end to make sure we touched and healed all the people.

W. V. Grant and all the other preachers I have had the honor to be with and learn from, I want to take this time to thank every one of you. *Amen.*

Always remember the word of knowledge is one of our creator's wonderful gifts.

Praise the Lord.

Chapter 8

My Home in Heaven out of Diamonds

Jesus' Exotic Garden

The Lord and I talked this all over about five years ago. It is how things are going to be in heaven for me and all of God's children. This is what is going to happen and the way I want to build this in heaven. This is for all the children all over the world who have never seen the Lord's creations.

There are roses and flowers all over the world that most people have never seen before. The Lord said this is what I'm going to be able to do in heaven. What we will do is take an area that is seven miles long and seven miles wide. Each section will be seven feet by seven feet, so you will have an area for miles of all the roses, and then the next one when you're going down the path will be all the different flowers. We will have trolley car where you can drive all the people down the paths with every different type of flower from all over the country so we all can see them. Each flower will have its own section of seven feet by seven feet. When we go through here with the trolley car for the people going down the gold streets, for all to see, the flowers will wave to you, tell you what type of flower they are, and tell you what country they came from.

The reason it will be seven feet by seven feet is because in the Bible seven is the Lord's number. It is the day the Lord rested.

Further on down the gold path, there will be all the different types of trees, and the same thing will take place. All the trees as you go by will introduce themselves and tell you where they are from and their name. When I was out in California, they have these huge redwood trees. I was in my van with my sailboat on the back; I drove up to this huge redwood tree where a man had carved a hole through the tree for cars to drive through. (*Wow!*) The Lord created all kinds of trees, for example, the oak tree, pine tree, maple tree, and so on, just so we could have all these types of trees to make planks, tables, and flooring.

The next path will be the fruit trees, with every fruit you could imagine that the Lord has put here on earth for us. As you go by, the same thing will take place. The fruit trees, will tell you the type of fruit that they are and where they came from. If you would like to pick a flower or a fruit to have, that's fine, because after you pick whatever you want, another one will take its place. You see, it will last forever. (Praise the Lord!) Now remember, the Lord just didn't make one type of apple tree; there are dozens of types of apples the Lord made, and they all will be there. Let's not forget the bushes, grapes, berries, corn all the types, and onions; it will all be the same. Oh yes, and even the weeds, such as the dandelions. Italian women stew them, and it's very good for you. When we drive down this gold path, all of the people who have never seen some of these things will be able to see them. What an amazing thing to take place up in heaven.

I will be determined to allow all of the Lord's children to see all of God's creations. I had an uncle who didn't get to see all of the things the Lord created, so imagine his face when he will be able to see all of the Lord's creation.

Up in heaven, there will be no gas engines or population problems. There will be gold wheels, and all you will have to do is speak to the trolley car and tell it slower or faster or tell it to go straight or make a left or right turn. How wonderful!

What an education we all will have to learn all of the Lord's flowers, trees, grapes, and let's not forget the orchids, my favorite flower. Why, you may ask, is the orchid my most favorite flower? Well, when I was a young man and I was going to see a girlfriend of mine, I stopped in at a florist's shop to see what type of flower to buy. I made the biggest mistake of my life; I was just going to buy her some candy. The guy at the florist shop said, "Why would you buy her candy? You need to buy her beautiful flowers, young man, if you want to get a message across to her."

So yes, I bought the most gorgeous orchids for her. I gave her the box, and she just went wild. I pinned the orchid on her, and we went out to dinner. The florist was right. People were walking up to us and commented on her flower, and she took me home and hugged and kissed me and kept on thanking me. This is why the orchid has been my favorite flower. It showed me love.

Praise the lord.

Let's All Help God's Children

The Lord and I were sitting on the front porch at the Jesus Miracle Chapel talking about all the material we had put into the church. When we first had started laying the concrete floors for the church, I had delivered to me two truckloads of sand, which is about eighteen tons a load. Talk about a mountain high! Boy oh boy, it was high, and about one thousand bags of cement. My trusty wheelbarrow, my little cement mixer, and I did the job. I would shovel all the sand and tear up all the cement mix and then roll it up the hill about seventy feet long and roll it across the driveway to my friend, who was laying the blocks at that time. I would haul it up to him on a scaffold in six-gallon buckets so he could use it to set the blocks.

This is how I believed I hurt all the cartilage in my knees. There were tons and tons of steel that I lifted up by hand. I had to chuckle when I told the Lord, "I do not want to see another cement block in my life." I should have never said that, because not long after that Hurricane Charlie and a tornado came through and blew it all down on me: the roof, the walls, everything was gone. I have pictures of it. I mean everything was gone.

I started to rebuild the church again; I was sixty-five when I started, and now at eighty-four, I am still rebuilding the church with no cartilage in my knees. Ken, a good friend of mine, came over every day to help the Lord and me. We would have never got as far as we did. Thanks to all the others who have helped the Lord and me with the building of the Jesus Miracle Chapel.

Now before I forget, Ken's lovely wife, Shirley, would bring us over lunch after putting in a Lord's day of hard work. Let me tell you about her cheesecake. It's out of this world. I would dream about her cheesecake and then go to the supermarket and buy some, but it just didn't compare to hers. I would have to give the rest of the store-bought cheesecake to my dog. I told Shirley that she should get a hold of some of the most famous bakeries and let them sample her cheesecake. God Bless Shirley and Ken for all they have done for our Lord and me.

I told the Lord, "I have done all this for you and would do it all over again."

The Lord told me, "My son, you built a house for me, and now let me tell you about the house for you, that I have built.

"Your house in heaven will not be cement blocks; it will be solid diamond blocks. They are thicker, a foot high and a foot wide, and six feet long, a solid diamond block."

I remember the biggest diamond they had on hand is called the "Cullinan Diamond," which means the holy star. The Lord said, "It is going to take over five thousand of those diamond blocks, my son. When I put them on top and tell them to stay, they will stay there."

I was completely flabbergasted with what he was telling me. The Lord told me, "I will put a roof over this, and you can use any type of material you want for the roof. It will be one solid piece of whatever you choose."

I guess it was in my spirit when I said to the Lord, "Lord, I want my roof top be an emerald roof, all one solid piece. If it's emerald and it is a bright, sunny day, can I change the color?"

The Lord said, "Yes, my son, you can do that."

Then I asked the Lord about the doors. "Lord, I like big, tall doors; some of the doors I have seen in big cathedrals are about nine feet high, and oval at the top. Lord, can you put that type of door in for me?"

The Lord said, "Yes, my son, I will put as many as you want." The Lord said each door would be a solid pearl.

"Wow," I said. "Lord, can you put a couple of black pearl doors for me?"

"Yes," He answered.

The Lord told me what I can do. He said, "These doors will open and close just by you speaking to them."

I said to the Lord, "Well, that will be wonderful, and Lord, when I was a young boy, we had those doorknobs that were round and made of glass, and they looked like diamonds. Can I have that?"

"Yes, my son, but it will just be for looks, because you walk up to the door and command it to open."

The Lord and I walk and talk all the time. I had put the TV on, and there was Oprah on TV, and the Lord and I were watching it. There was a young teenage girl on the show with an artificial arm that cost 4 million dollars, and it ran on batteries, with electrical wires that ran up to her brain. She told Oprah, "All I have to do is think of which way I want my arm to go, and with the brain waves, it will do as I command."

Oprah told the young lady, "Well then think of your arm going up."

The young lady said, "Okay, I will think of my arm going up," and I'll be it when right up. It was wonderful, and I was so happy to see this. Oprah always has wonderful shows, and I never miss her shows.

The Lord said to me, "Son, I changed my mind. Remember when I told you to command the door to open? Well, after watching the Oprah show with you, I like the fact that you just have to think it, so it will be done. However, Son, there will be no batteries connected to your brain. You just have to think it, and it shall open."

The Lord was sitting here with me at all times, watching me and telling me all that I have written. You see, I wrote this entire book by hand. I do not type; I gave all the writings to a very close friend, who has taken the time and effort to type all of the great miracles, and my personal walk and talk with the Lord. Bless her and her family, and all the others who have donated their time to help. God bless.

The Lord, who is standing here right beside me, says this is parallel with the Bible. I said, "What do you mean?"

"Well, I told all the disciples what to write in the Bible, and now I am telling you. I have reminded you of all the miracles you and I have done, and worked together with. I just do not want you to forget them."

Now let me make this clear; we work together with the Lord. I, with all these miracles, would lay my hand on all of these people and pray for these people. The Lord did the healing. I could not heal anything. The Lord is the healer. The Lord told me this is the best book ever written beside the Bible. I said, "Why, Lord?"

The Lord said, "Because it is all about me."

I would like to make sure that half of the royalties from this go to all of Oprah's children.

I have dedicated my whole life, and all of my earthly goods, to our Lord. All that I have done for our Lord will remain in my mind and heart forever.

My next goal is to finish the Jesus Miracle Chapel and to leave another pastor to run it while I travel all over the world to see all the vets and pray and talk to them and tell them about the Lord; this is my next wish. Lord, I pray that this will come true.

Praise the Lord

Let's keep our children safe.
Photo taken by Mary Stauffer

The Gold Sailboat

Sailing, sailing, sailing. I really love it and have been privileged to do more that my share. I even wrote a book on sailing. After this most fantastic story, I might briefly tell you about it and my experiences, which are extremely interesting, but now let us get back to the gold sailboat.

I was sitting on the front porch of the chapel one morning early, just Jesus and me. We were talking about heaven, and I mentioned to Jesus that I would sure love to have a sailboat in heaven. He said, "Sure, Son." Wow, was he so agreeable. I told him I would like one about sixty-four feet long. He said, "No, Son, it will be seventy-four feet long." He sure likes to give you more than you expect or want. I have no idea what the sailboat would be made of, as I have made many boats myself in three of my own factories out of steel, aluminum, and fiberglass. I was more than surprised when Jesus told me it was going to be out of solid gold, not regular gold as we know it, but transparent gold, clear as glass. It will be the same gold as Jesus and I walked on the gold streets of heaven on the cover of my book.

If you have time someday, look at Revelations 21:21. That is the first time I ever heard of a reference with the chapter and the verse the same. It tells you about the clear gold like glass. I have been down to Key West, where they have a boat they take you out for a ride in called the glass-bottom boat. You can see all the fish below it, and the fish love popcorn. The pilot of the boat said the fish know the sound of the boat's motor, and that is the reason they follow the boat. I was so thrilled, so I asked Jesus if I could have a large silver sail on the gold sailboat, as I have a wooden sailboat with a clock in the center, and it has beautiful silver sails. It is a piece you set on your table, just about a foot and a half long. The gold sailboat has no motor or fuel, as most boats do, to get them into the harbor or from dock to dock. This is the way you control the boat.

Jesus said very clearly, "Son just speak it, and whatever you want it to do, it will do as you command. If you want the boat to go a little faster, you just instruct the wind to kick up a little, or the same it you want it to go slower. If you want your sailboat to go left or right, you do the same thing; you speak it, and it shall be done. Now get this—you can even tell it to go backward or even tell the boat to come to a complete stop. This process will surely come in handy when you want to dock your boat.

Wow! Complete control just by telling it what to do. Now, I have been on many of the large cruise ships. They are noted for their wonderful food. At breakfast, I would order lots of bacon, sausage, and pancakes. In the evening, there are beautiful white tablecloths and about twenty waiters, all coming in at the same time with flaming trays. At lunch, they had about forty feet of tables around the swimming pool with a complete variety of foods to choose from. This was just amazing with all the variety of foods to choose from to eat and enjoy.

Now on to the golden sailboat. You will find no food in it at all. You will find a stack of gold plates and cut diamond glasses for drinking. Everyone picks up their plate and hollow diamond glass, walks over to where they want to eat, and sits down. The first thing I asked Jesus was if they all have little gold tables to set their plates on. Jesus said, "No, just put the plate in the air at your desired height and it will stay there."

There will be fifty people on the boat, and we all like different meals. Whatever you want to eat, just speak it, and it will appear on your plate. I told Jesus I wanted meatloaf, mashed potatoes and gravy, corn, peas, and a crescent roll with butter and some strawberry jam. I asked Jesus what he wanted for the main course, and he showed me the clearest vision I have ever seen and will never forget. It was a very large piece of bright pink salmon. I still carry that clear vision of the salmon, and I always will.

Now we are ready for dessert, so you just say, "Plate be clean," and it will be sparkling clean. I said, "I want a piece of that German chocolate cake, a piece of cherry pie, and two scoops of French vanilla ice cream," and I would actually see it appear. I asked Jesus what he wanted for dessert. Now this is the greatest compliment my dear mother ever had, and it came right from Jesus' lips. Jesus said, "Your dear mother used to make the best lemon pie with meringue on top," and he reminded me at the family picnic they would say, "Mary, you just bring a couple of those large lemon pies." Jesus said, "That's what I want for my dessert, one of those delicious lemon pies of your mother's." Thank you, Jesus, and I hope you let her hear you say that in heaven; it will be the time of her life. Now, I have had this talk and vision personally so many times, and it becomes more real every time. Maybe the best is yet to follow.

We will all gather around Jesus and hear him speak. He told me he was not going to preach; he was going to teach. What I am hoping to have is a question-and-answer service. There are questions I and a lot of my friends, and other true believers, will want to know about something that is in the Holy Bible. God talks about a certain person, and his name is Melchizedek. The hypothesis is that he was without beginning and without end, without mother or father; even Abraham had to pay him.

I understand that God could create him without a mother or father and there does not have to be an end—it can go on forever and ever—but most things have a beginning, and he must have had a beginning when God created him. Won't it be great to have the Master answer all of the questions we have always wondered about?

I must state this is not going to be just a one-time weekend event but will go on for millions, and billions of years. Who knows? Maybe you will all have your turn to ride on the golden sailboat with Jesus and have your favorite meal. It may be sooner than we think.

Praise the Lord.

Chapter 9

New Fragrance, Thirty-Nine Stripes

Lee Hoffman
Sphinx of Giza
Jerusalem Pyramid

Lee's Greatest Wish and Desire Will Come True Kissing Jesus' Back

Many people have asked me, "Now that you, Lee, have had so many wonderful personal experiences and so many one-on-one talks with our Creator and Savior of the world, what would be your greatest pleasure and personal desire?" I have told a few that the good Lord has already talked it over with me and went into complete detail about what and how it was to take place, and I am so thrilled that he, Jesus, actually confirmed that he was willing to personally participate in this wish and longtime dream of mine. What a thrill to know it is for sure going to happen and to look forward to that wonderful and perfect day that will be the one and only greatest day that could ever happen to me and I can say for anyone who has loved our Lord Jesus. Nothing has happened like this before or will ever happen in the future. I believe, and I am positive after you read about it, you and the whole world will finally agree with me.

Jesus and I were sitting on the porch of the chapel as we both discussed the situation and both agreed on every minute detail. Isn't it wonderful when the Lord and you agree completely to the very last, intimate details and when I am in heaven with him, Jesus?

He dropped over to my house, the way he previously told me he would, exactly how he was going to build it out of solid diamond blocks the size of our cement blocks. Jesus agreed to come after prayer, lay down on my bed, and expose his back and shoulders down to the waist as he lies naturally on his stomach. Jesus went into the way he was going to invent, or I should say create, a new kind of oil that has never been created. Jesus explained to me the first ingredient was a *rose* since one of his names is the Rose of Sharon. The next one is going to be lilies, as Jesus' name is also Lily of the Valley. I believe it was me who mentioned orchids. Jesus agreed those three would make the finest fragrance ever. This new oil will smell like the combination of these three flowers.

Jesus then explained to me how he would touch my hand, and they would be strong but as smooth as a newborn baby, and when I poured the oil on his back and massaged it in, it would be so very smooth. After I gave him a complete massage on his back to his waist and around his shoulders and neck, the best part starts to begin. With his back dripping with this precious oil and the fragrance permeating the entire room and house, I then would have the biggest desire of my heart; I would now be able to **kiss** my Savior's back. I would gently lower my lips into the oil and move my lips over his whole back, shoulders, and neck. I would kiss and kiss my Master's back, on which he took the thirty-nine stripes, as you might have seen in the Jesus movie. What a thrill—what an honor, what a privilege.

My dream is now taking place, and I realize I am the most-honored person at this time in all of heaven. As all of this conversation taking place on the front porch of the chapel, at the end of our time and prayer, I head for my trailer, which I have lived in for many years. As I opened the door and stepped in, I instantly smelled the fabulous fragrance. As the old saying goes, you could cut it with a knife. It became reality. After I had taken about seven steps, Jesus confirmed that the fragrance I smelled was the same as it would be when kissing his back.

Yes, many people have dreams and imaginative thoughts, but it is different when the King of Kings and the Lord of Lords sits next to you and calls you son and tells you personally that it is definitely going to happen. It is then confirmed by putting that same fragrance in my trailer and then telling me that is what it will smell like when I am in the middle of kissing his beautiful, precious, sweet, darling back. He suffered for the whole world, but the whole world does not appreciate it the way they should.

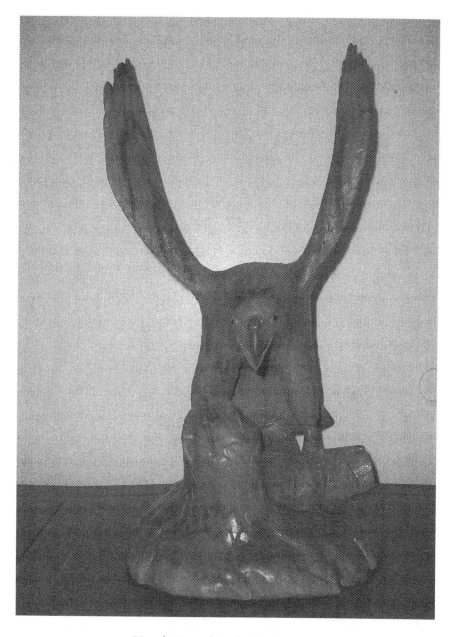

Hand-Carved in the Philippines
Last Piece of Rose Wood

Chapter 10

Relationship I Have with Jesus

Riding Camel in Jerusalem
Lee Hoffman

Both Sides of the River

The Lord and I have talked many times about this subject for over twenty years. Some of you folks may have never heard of the expression before, including many Christians either.

It's called both sides of the river. You ask what that means. Well, let me explain.

You get on one side of the river, which means you're on the other side. The other side of the river means the secular side, where you're working, playing, having a good time, buying big homes, and paying into the stock market. Now that's all the wonderful things that happen, and *praise the Lord,* I'm glad it does happen for most of the people. That's called being on the other side of the river. (Laughs.)

This is what they call this side of the river. It's not about your home, working, playing, or having a good time; it's *spiritual.* You have lived two lives on both sides of the river. You've lived the secular life with all the little goodies, yachts, cars, houses, stocks, etc. ... and now you live this one with the *spiritual life.* When the Lord told me this, it kind of startled me a little bit, and it may startle you too. The Lord says, "There is nobody on planet earth who has lived a great life such as I have lived." The Lord went on to explain this was true even those who wrote the Bible: Matthew, Luke, Mark, John, Peter, Paul. Paul wrote two-thirds of the New Testament. Everybody preaches, "Paul said this and Paul said that, and Paul is a great man," because he wrote two-thirds of the Bible. That was on one side of the river, but he never was on the other side of the river, because those guys at that time didn't have any money. All they had were sandals, and dirt would get into their feet after they had preached and done all those great things.

Jesus took thirty-nine stripes across his back, a very hard lashing. Most people don't know why he took thirty-nine stripes. The way the Bible states it is that it's forty minus one. The reason it's forty minus one is because if the guy who is whipping you makes a mistake and misses you, then he gets forty. They whipped Jesus and tore up his back. This is what Jesus took on his back; he shed his blood for all the sins of the world. Paul states that he took the lashing five different times. That's five times thirty-nine slashes on his back. You can just imagine what his back looked like. After all that, he asked Jesus, "Can you heal my eyes?" Jesus said *no*. Later he asked Jesus the same thing, "Can you heal my eyes?" Jesus again said, *"No, my grace is sufficient for thee."* Then they cut his head off. In some places in Rome, people say they still have his head. It was not a very good life they had.

The Lord started to remind me of all the good things I have had. He said, "You've had more Cadillacs, convertible Cadillacs, Fleetwood Cadillacs, and Red Biarritz Cadillacs than anybody I know of. You had about thirty-five yachts, about five of the biggest sailboats, the fastest sailboat, the most classic cars, motorcycles, huge mansions, summer homes, a beautiful home down in Boca Raton, and the best pool in town. You've had all these things, and you have traveled the world." On one vacation trip, I spent nearly $73,000. There was a big write-up on it in the Detroit news about how I spent $73,000.

Then the Lord said to me, "On the other side of the river, my son, not very many people have had the life you have had. If they did have that life on that side of the river, on this side of the river not too many good things have happened to them." The Lord said to me that because of the combination of these things, "No one has lived like you, because on the other side of the river, you have had more money. A lot of people have not seen a thousand-dollar bill. The biggest maybe is a hundred-dollar bill." At the time I was well-off financially, thousand-dollar bills were very popular, and I always had my pockets stuffed.

The Lord has told me, "You see, my son, you have lived ten times better than most on planet earth." This is why he reminded me of all the good things I had on the other side of the river. The Lord said, "The other thing is that now you're on this side of the river, which is the spiritual side, so you have to add them together. There are a lot of preachers who have been preaching for ten to fifteen years and have never had most of the things you have had. For example, walking on the gold streets with me, having me come into your bedroom and take you out of your bed, your shadow healings, praying for people, millions of miracles, and the things you are writing in this book. There is no one who has experienced and witnessed all the things you have with me."

The Lord continued, "Personally, I never grabbed anyone else and held their hand thousands of times. You and I have a closer relationship than anyone else." The Lord said this is why I need to combine all these things from both sides of the river. He said, "You have led your life ten times better than anybody else. Some people have led their lives on one side of the river really well, and some not so well, so when you combine the two, no one has had the relationship you and I have had."

I told the Lord, "Well, I'm glad to talk this over with you, but I don't want people to think I'm bragging." The Lords said, *"No,* my son, you put this in. This is my personal walk and talk with you." A lot of people don't know what both sides of the river are, so this will be a wonderful education for them. It may help in their faith to know this. Some of the people who are on the other side of the river, may want to come over spiritual to get a taste of this side of the river.

The Lord said to me, "Son, repeat to me the first verse you ever learned in the Bible."

I replied, "Yes, Lord, it's Mark 8:36."

Then the Lord said, "Well, my son, then call it out."

I said, "Okay, Lord: 'For what shall it profit a man, if he shall gain the whole world, and lose his own soul?' Lord, that is quite a verse."

The Lord said, "Well let me explain that to you."

I told the Lord, "You don't have to explain it to me. I know what it's all about."

Lord said, "No I'm going to explain something to you. I could have made that verse, 'For what shall it profit, if he gains all the gold, and silver, and lose his own soul?' I wanted to come on stronger than that. I want to gain the world, the whole country, all the gold, silver, and buildings, everything in the whole world if you gained it all."

I said, *"Wow!* That's really coming on strong, Lord.

The Lord said, "My son, that's what I wanted to do. People who read this, if they have had a wonderful life on the other side of the river, and there are lots of people who are multi-billionaires, will be interested. 'For what shall it profit a man, if he shall gain the whole word, and lose his own soul?' A lot of these billionaires don't have time to come to my side of the river. They are too wrapped up in their lives and the stock markets or whatever else they do. They really need to take the time to seek me and see how spiritually they can be with me."

I hope this really does help and that now you know there are two sides of the river. As I stated, you came into this world with nothing on, and you will leave with nothing on. This is the way both sides of the river will go out. You see, it really doesn't matter what side you're on, because you will go out the way you were born—naked.

I PRAY AND HOPE THAT YOU DO COME OVER AND CHECK OUT THE SPIRITUAL SIDE OF THE RIVER.

I'D LIKE TO CLOSE THIS WITH A WONDERFUL VERSE:

> Whatsoever you do in this whole world shall come to pass, but only what you do for Christ will last.

The Lord brought up this subject himself. He said to me, "Son, some of my best friends, my best disciples, have walked with me for two years, some three and a half years. I lived for thirty-three and a half years and that was a short time that some of walked and talked with me. You know you have been walking and talking with me for seventy years. You're eighty-four years old now, and for approximately the last seventy years, you have been walking and talking with me." Then the Lord sort of caught me off guard and said, "You know, twice my age would be sixty-seven years, and if I lived twice that long, you have still lived and walked and talked with me two lifetimes."

I told the Lord, "That's very nice of you, but my big prayer and life today is that I can live till the rapture, and serve you the best I can right now till the rapture. When I'm up there with you, Lord, I want to serve you and be your sidekick. I will really take care of everything you want me to do here and up there."

The Lord told me, "Son, don't be afraid to be challenged anywhere, in public or on TV; I'll be right by your side if someone doesn't believe you!"

Praise the Lord!

W or W

Now this is a cute little story the Lord and I have talked about many times. It will give me pleasure to share and to tell all of the Lord's children this one.

Now you might ask what w or w stands for. It stands for worship or weight.

When we eat food, it can go to two sources. It can give you strength to worship the Lord. Alternatively, it can give you strength to put on fat.

I have a picture of me from many, many years ago in a little red, tiny swimsuit. My hair had not turned white at that time. It still was dark. I have showed this picture to many people now and tell them I am sixty-five in that one. They look at it in awe and say, "You cannot be sixty-five. You look to be in your late forties." I can confess that I eat a lot of donuts, French fries, burgers, candy bars, cherry pies, and ice cream. I worked in Detroit downtown when I was young and had cherry pie with ice cream every day for two years and never missed a day.

With all of the sweets and fast foods I have eaten, I should probably be one hundred pounds overweight. I have never let anything touch my lips without praising the Lord. It does not matter what it is, whether it is a bottle of water, can of soda, or even a stick of gum, I make sure I praise the Lord. I might of mention this before people go into a fast food restaurant and never bow their head before they eat. It does not matter if you are in a fancy restaurant or a fast food place, you should bow your head to praise our Lord. This is nothing to be ashamed of to praise the Lord before you eat. I am eighty-four now, and I think within the last twenty years I have doubled up on all the goodies, and I still maintain my weight.

As I stated, in the beginning worship or weight, always praise the Lord.

Praise the Lord.

Vision

I have dedicated my life to pray and bless all of the Lord's children all over the world. I have prayed for millions of miracles. I have counseled people for over forty thousand hours. These people include all the police department, fire departments, etc. I have never asked for or taken a single donation for my work. I do not draw a wage, and I do not charge people for counseling. I know two Christian counselors who charge $150 an hour and have people waiting months to see them. I give people all the time they need, at no charge, and see them whenever they need to be seen.

Recently I had to have surgery on my eyes. I went over to see the doctors. They are the most wonderful people, and I have met. They schedule me for my operations, and they said, "We have three different types here, and you need to pick one." I have Medicaid, and Medicare, and the first one Medicaid will pay for, but it is not a very good implant. The second implant, which is a little better, will cost around $600 per eye, and I will be able to see a little better with that. The third implant, if you want to see distances, or further away, will cost $2,000 per eye. (Wow $4,000!) I told the doctor I could not afford that and I'd have to take the free one. Before the operation, I had to get eye drops, so the doctor gave me a prescription for it. I took the prescription over to a big pharmacy, and they told me for the eye drops it was going to cost $96 and for the other one prescription it would be $77. I could not afford that. I decided to go back to my doctor and tell him that I could not afford these drops. I went back and told him, "I cannot afford this. We need to cancel the operation." The doctor said, "Oh no, I will give you drops that I have here." I thanked him, and I took them.

I was watching the president-elect on TV, and he stated that we would all have the best insurance. That sounds good to me. I watched him, his lovely wife, and his beautiful girls. If they had to go in for eye problems, I know he would want them to have the best. I know he would tell the doctor he wanted the very best for his two children. He would tell the doctor that their vision is the most important thing for them. He would not want the surgery that is free—no one would—and we all know that our vision is very important to us. This goes for all the vice presidents, congressmen, and lawyers. You know you would want the best for your family.

We all are supposed to be the Lord's children, and the Lord wants us all to have the very best of vision or medical care when needed. If you have loads of money, well then money talks, and you can pay for the very best. When it comes to a poor preacher man like me, who has dedicated his life for our Lord, you do not get the very best. You get whatever you can afford at that time. This is how working-class people who don't have enough money, like me, get the bum rap. You people are spending billions of dollars and throwing out the red carpet to people, and then people like us have to get the cheap end of this raw deal. This is how the Lord's children are treated.

Praise the Lord.

Money, Money, Money
Where Does It Come From?

Jesus and I were watching a television program exposing some wealthy ministries. I am going to elaborate on this subject.

One preacher drives a Rolls Royce automobile, which he stated costs over $200,000. He also has a new helicopter, and I think it was priced at around 1.5 million or so. I might be off a million, but you see where I am going with this. I said to the Lord, "Where in the world does he get all that money?" The Lord said, "Son, where do you think he gets it? *Out of the collection plate.*"

One major minister said he could not be bothered flying on a regular commercial plane even if he flew in first class and has his own jet and limousines. He has flown around the world a few times and had never even flown first-class.

I always went coach and always got to talk with others about Jesus, my favorite confirmation.

The preacher said his wife had about two hundred pairs of expensive shoes and he had about a dozen very expensive suits or more. I said to the Lord, "Where in the world does he get all that money?" The Lord said, "Son, where do you think he gets it? *Out of the collection plate.*" Some live in million-dollar homes and take $75,000 vacations.

I will not mention their names or the names of their churches or ministries. I know their pictures have been on the television. They have been exposed, but they just do not care. I actually heard one of them on television tell the congregation, "If you believe as I do and lead the kind of life I do, you could all have the same." *Give me a break!* They do not all have a collection plate they can dip their hands in. Maybe some families in the congregation just were laid off from their jobs, which they held for twenty years or more, and are still trying to make house payments and car payments.

They go to church and listen to all that high and mighty talk. I have even heard the pastor say if you have written out your check and do not think is large enough, just tear it up and write out a larger one. Yeah, write a larger one, because my new jet is costing a lot more than I thought to keep up!

I told Jesus, "I read in your book where you want us to be good stewards of God's money. That certainly does not sound like being a good steward of God's money to me." Thank goodness for television and the press for the way they have exposed these ministries. They are so brazen, they even brag to their own congregation of how much money they spend and the extravagant lifestyle they live. I could go on and on with plenty of material on this subject, but I have written enough about them to turn my stomach, so I will just call it complete for now.

Praise the Lord.

Chapter 11

He Said You're Really Going to Need Him, Followed
by I Believe the Greatest Miracle on Planet Earth.
Jesus Said, "I Did It as a Personal Favor"

Father God Gave Me all Power on Earth
Taiwan Convention

Tribute to Billy Graham

In this book, you may have noticed two Christmas cards from Billy Graham and his family. I would like to tell you all a little story about the cards. It was about twenty years ago, when the Jesus Miracle Chapel was called World Bible Explosion. That is when Billy Graham sent me the cards. When I started to build the chapel is when the Lord came to me and said, *"Son,* I believe we should name this the Jesus Miracle Chapel." I found these two pictures from Billy Graham after the hurricane. I am sure there is more from him, but I could not find them.

Billy Graham is one of the great preachers. He is well known around the world. He has preached in more countries, and for more people, than most other preachers. I saw him on TV a few nights ago. They played movies of Billy Graham when he was very young, right in his prime of life. It looks like he was in Australia preaching. I have never heard a more wonderful sermon in my life. I really wish I could have had that tape. It was just fabulous the way he was up there preaching to the people. He had what you would call a saving ministry. In other words, he was preaching to get the people saved.

I have done a lot of preaching in all the prisons over the world. I was a guest preacher at many churches and house meetings at people's homes where there were thirty to forty people. I have held several services on the front porch here at the Jesus Miracle Chapel. My ministry is part teaching, but it is mainly a miracle ministry. I told Father God, "I want miracle ministries like your son, Jesus." I was blessed to have the wonderful ministry I have.

I have had people ask me when I started laying hands on people. I said, "Exactly seventy years ago." I am eighty-four years old now, and the first person was my stepfather. He was lying in bed, and I laid my hands on him. Praise the Lord, he did get well. Now let's get back to Billy Graham's compassion to me. The greatest miracle in the world is being saved. Billy Graham has preached to millions of people around the world, and millions of people were saved. He has more involvement than I do or any other preacher that I know. It gives me great pleasure to show him a little acknowledgment in our book. Mr. Graham just recently celebrated his ninetieth birthday. I just hope and pray he lasts to the rapture.

One of my first books will go to Billy Graham and his son, Franklin. Franklin has taken over now for his father and is just doing a wonderful job. Franklin gives food all over the world for the Lord's children.

Billy, we love you, and when I get the chance, I would be honored to come out there to see you and your family again.

Thanks again. We love you.

May the Lord save us all.

During this
ous season, may the
st of Christmas bring
to you His peace, hope,
and joy.

Our Children
Gigi, Bunny, Anne, Franklin, Ned

"Fear not;

for, behold, I bring you good tidings
of great joy, which shall be to all
people. For unto you is born this day
in the city of David a Savior, who is
Christ the Lord."

Luke 2: 10-11

God bless you.

Preach in Tin Hut in Philippines

Tin Hut

Preach in Tin Hut in Philippines

A most wonderful Chinese woman named Nora Lamb wrote the famous book *China Cry*. It was made into a movie, which was directed by James F. Collier. Part of the movie that was famous was when they had her lined up in front of a firing squad to shoot her, and that's when the Lord had all the bullets miss her.

Nora and I are great friends. We went into China and smuggled eighty suitcases of Bibles and had services there. When we left China, I made sure that I gave enough money for them to build a church. Then we moved onto the Philippines, where we had services in a little tin hut, which was in Manila. We took roughly four Jeeps back through there, down muddy roads, where we came upon a little town. As we went through this little town, we saw small wood houses that looked like little shacks. The muddy roads were getting worse and worse until finally the Jeeps could progress no further. We all got out of the Jeeps and started to walk. We walked on some grass on the side of the muddy ruts in the dirt roads. We walked for about a half mile, and then we made it to the little tin building. Praise the Lord, they were all expecting us and even had a nice welcome sign posted.

I have pictures for my proof. I am going to explain to you to the best of my ability the way it was inside the little tin hut. The floor was all mud; there was not a piece of wood at all. The chairs were of all sorts, some kitchen, some straight chairs, benches, and old living room chairs, anything you could sit on. Some of the little round spindle legs were nearly two inches in the mud. The preacher, who looked to be in his twenties, and his wife showed me where they slept, which was on a pile of hay behind the altar. Now let me tell you about the restrooms. They furnish you with a shovel and a roll of toilet paper. You walk about three hundred feet behind the church and then, you guessed it, dig your own private hole, do your business, and then fill the hole back in with your shovel.

The great thing about it was the way this young preacher was so exuberant about his little church, and the way his wife and him slept behind the altar on a stack of hay.

I was so filled with compassion for this preacher and his wife that I reached into my pocket and took out all the money I had, which was really worth quite a bit more in their country, especially at that time. I put it all in someone's hat and then passed it all around to the other people who were with us. Thank you, Lord, it was enough money to buy building materials to build a nice little church and some chairs and of course, a wonderful wood floor. Boy, it made me feel so good before I left, knowing I left smiles on all their faces.

Oh yes, I have to mention this. Since they knew we were coming, they had cold colas waiting for us. It sure did taste good in that hot weather after walking in the mud all the way.

God bless our good brother and his faithful wife.

I would like to mention that I did become good friends with Nora Lamb's husband and their son. Mr. Lamb and I talked quite a bit about business. I explained to him about some inventions I knew of. We talked all about it, and he said to me, "Can you still make that?" I told him, "Why *yes!*" He said, *"Wow,* I would love to go into business with you. This sounds like it could make us millions of dollars."

This is what we talked about, and I will try to remember it word for word. Back in Detroit, I was a sales manager for a car company, and my best friend's name was Gilbert. Everyone called him Gil. He was the used car sales manager. Today they have an office with a glass case and desk, but years ago, it was like a shed in the car lot. In the wintertime, he would have a little radio and heater. One night it was cold, and Gil was in the shed,

159

and it was late evening. A guy came in with a black overcoat on, and said, "I have something here I would like to show you." Gil, being the kind of person he is, said, "Why sir, what do you have?"

The man opened up his long black overcoat, and there were about eight bottles in it. He said, "You see, those bottles are my inventions."

Gil was balder than bald, and of course, Gil said, "Can I try that?"

The man answered, "Why sure you can." The guy put some on Gil's hair and said, "I'll be back to check on you." Well I will be, Gil got thick, thick hair, and it just grew. He told me about it, and I would have never believed it until I saw it. Gil had a dog named Brownie, and he wanted to put some on his dog to see if it worked, and it did.

The person told Gil that this medicine was good for sinuses, so we tried it on the dog. We put some on a Q-tip and put it up on Brownie's nose, and Brownie loved it. Gil became good friends with this man and asked him how to make this medicine. The old man said, "Gil, you have been so wonderful to me helping me out, so I will tell you." He told Gil how to make this hair-growing medicine, from some kind of a bush.

When Gil went back over to see him, he found the old man had passed away in his bed. The man's wife gave Gil the rest of the bottles that were left. Gil thought so much of me and gave me his gold he had gotten for being employee of the year. He said to me, "I want to take you down an eight-mile road in Detroit and give you a sauna bath."

When I came out, he gave me cedar branches. I said okay and slapped myself with the branches. After that, we went about two miles down the road and went to the bar, and I had a big cheeseburger. Gil said to me, "I want to tell you how to make this medicine. I trust you, Lee, and I want you to know." When Gil passed away, his wife called me and asked me if I could be one of the pallbearers. I asked his wife where the bottles were, and she said, "That trash? I threw it all away." Later I wanted to try to see if it would work. I went and got the cedar branch and made it up, took it, and put it in my hair, and it did grow. That is why Nora Lamb's husband and I were going to go into business together.

Now off to Taiwan. This is another great miracle. We had a revival in an indoor arena. I would guess the place was packed, and there were nearly twenty thousand people there, plus myself, of course, and four other preachers. At the far end, there was a scaffold where the people would walk up and across to the preachers. The preachers had the anointing oil, and when the people would walk through, the preachers would put the anointing oil on their foreheads to anoint them. I have done this many times over the world, so I wanted to get right out in the middle of the arena where the people were. I have a photo of this. I have no clue who took it or where it came from, but Lord, I do have a picture of me in the middle of the arena, with my hands up in the air. You might ask why. Father God, in a stern voice, put his hand on my left shoulder and squeezed it so hard, and said, "Son I give you all power in heaven and earth."

I looked up and threw my arms up in the air, which is what is in the photo. I replied, "Why that's what you told your son Jesus—that you give him all power and earth."

Father God said, "Yes, my son, and now I give it to you." Father God told me that I was going to need it; yes, that is what he said.

I believe I did have the power of Jesus. I do not doubt Father God's word. If he says I have all power in heaven and earth, I truly do believe it. Therefore, for nearly two hours, I had all the power of heaven and earth. People were packed around me so tight, like in New York, where you cannot even move. Because of this, Father God parted the people, just as he did with the red sea. He opened a path for me around eighty feet long and thirty feet wide. I then walked down the middle of them all, and as I did this, my shadow followed me and touched all the people.

There were people throwing up. I have never seen so much vomit. There were men throwing up on the women. It was the demons coming out of them all. I got to the end, and there was a woman with a little boy who was around five years of age with steel braces on his legs who could not walk. I asked the woman, "Has he ever walked?"

She replied, "No, never."

I told her, "Just stay there. Let's see if we can make him walk."

I stuck out my forefinger on my left hand, and he grabbed a hold of it. I walked him back with me with his steel braces going click, click, click down the path that Father God had made for me. The little boy who had never walked started walking down the path with me.

As I walked back, I saw the most beautiful woman I had ever seen. I believe she was from Malaysia. She had a green Chinese outfit on and beautiful eyes, and her complexion was not like marble. It looked like pure porcelain, white as white can be. There were no pores in it at all. She followed me as I walked the little boy back, and when I got done walking the little boy back, they rushed up a lady about seventy-five years old who had milky eyes and could not see. I placed my hand on her shoulder, and said, "You can see." She had beautiful blue eyes.

The woman in the green outfit came up to me and said, "Touch me, please."

I said, "My child, what is wrong with you? You look beautiful to me."

She reached up with her hands and moved her long black hair from around her neck and my Lord, and she had something that looked like two goiters on each side of her neck. They were as nearly big as a football, with blood coming out the back of them. I touched her on the shoulder and said, "Depart, my child," and just as I did that, the preachers came up to me and said the bus was there and we had to leave, so I didn't see if I had healed her on not. As we were leaving, there was a young girl running to me who was trying to get to me. I do not know why, but Father God picked her up, turned her around, and threw her in the air like an arrow. I had never in my life seen anything like this.

We all went back to the hotel, and we had the most beautiful room. There was a living room, bar, kitchen, and dining room. My roommate got up in the morning and went to the window and pulled back the brown velvet drapes, and the sun poured right through. He said to me, "You better get up and go get breakfast."

I said, "Okay, I'll be right there."

Then the greatest miracle happened. As I was sitting up in my bed, Jesus was standing there with the young girl who had the goiters on her neck. Jesus stood there at the foot of my bed with his big hands and removed the hair from the young girl. Jesus said, "See, my son, they are gone; I wanted to come back and bring her here for you to see that she was healed." Imagine that, Jesus. What a wonderful Lord we have.

Something similar to that took place in the United States. I had run an ad in a very popular Christian magazine called *Charisma* near where I live in Boca Rotan. The ad was around $250, so I drove there to pay for it. The nice woman took the money and said, "It was nice of you to drive here to pay for this." The young woman said she was getting ready to leave and asked if I'd like to join her for a steak dinner. I said, "Sure, wow that would be a great honor."

I followed her to a delicious steak house, and we sat down to eat. All this is very interesting, so pay attention. When we were almost done with our steak dinner, she told me about a church in Orlando that was having a service that night and asked if I would like to join her. I said, "Why sure." The speaker was with Benny Hinn. I was in this church many years ago. I remember I had a white silk suit on with my gold cross and a red tie. Benny Hinn was on the altar stage and pointed to me. he said, "Hey you, sir, are you a preacher?"

I replied, "Could be."

He invited me up to the altar, so I went. Mr. Hinn talked with me and asked me, "What are you doing?" so I told him that I was going to China, Taiwan, and the Philippines with Nora Lamb. What a wonderful preacher. He put his arms around me and said, "Everybody in this church, raise your hands and let us pray for this remarkable man for all the Lord's work that he is doing." They all prayed for me.

A few months later, Mr. Hinn invited me back and had me back on the altar. I was sitting in a gold chair with Mr. Hinn, and we all listened to his sermon. After the sermon, he went out the back door.

I walked toward the altar, and there was this young American boy who was five years old, just like the Taiwanese boy whose miracle I had witnessed. I asked his mother, "Can he walk?"

She replied, "Why, no."

I tried the same thing on him I had tried on the other little boy. I took my left hand again and had him pull on the fourth finger and walked that little boy just like the little boy in Taiwan. What a wonderful Lord we have.

There was a nice couple there in their twenties, and I asked the young man, "Can you walk without the crutches?" Father God told me to take his crotches and give them to the young lady and take the young man and run and dance around the church. Father God healed him too.

What a wonderful time I had there with Benny Hinn. There were many miracles that took place.

It gives me great pleasure to put all of these wonderful miracles together for all to read.

Praise the Lord.

I would like to close this with a little story about Nora Lamb. I live near St. Cloud, Florida, and in a little town near there called Kissimmee, Florida, they were having a banquet for Nora Lamb. When I found out about this, I bought a ticket to go, I arrived a little late, but thank the Lord, I made it. I got a great seat close to the stage, and I was listening to Nora give a talk about someone who had hit her in the head I believe it was with a two-by-four, and it had knocked her out. She claims that she has been dizzy every since it had happened. To see Nora again—wow. She talked about how she had to stand in front of a firing squad and the bullets all missed her. Then someone came along and beat her over the head with a two-by-four. I was watching her, and she looked like she was going to fall over, so I jumped up on the stage and grabbed her so she would not fall over. With the microphone still in her hand, she took one look at me and said, "Folks, this is the preacher who took care of me in China, the Philippines, Taiwan, and all over the place."

I should tell you Nora is the one who gave me the name Preacher Man, and it has stuck with me since. Nora and I sat down, and after all those years, she remembered me. What a joy. It made me feel so proud.

Praise the Lord.

Nora Lamb and Preacher Man Lee Hoffman.

Chinese Prisoners Making Dinner

Children Prisoners in China

More Prison Camps

Rapture Tribulation Millennium

One of my favorite verses in the Bible is the one that talks about not concentrating on what you have and see in this world but to keep your mind elevated for the world to come. Of course, that is what I have done. I have been fortunate to be in heaven and to be with the Lord and have him talk to me about my new home and things of that nature.

What I am going to do now is talk about the millennium. This happens a thousand years after the tribulation. I have talked to many people about the rapture and asked them, "Do you know what the rapture means?"

They reply, "Rapture? What is that?"

Some of these people are in their twenties, and some are older than that. They all do not know what the rapture is. I say, "You know the anointing. Do you know what the anointing means?"

"No, no," they all say.

"Well, have you read your Bible at all?" I ask.

"No, not really," they reply.

Let me give you a brief idea of what comes before the millennium. First comes the rapture and then the seven-year tribulation. The seven-year tribulation is divided into two forty-two-month periods. The first forty-two months is called the tribulation, and the last forty-two months is called the great tribulation. The way the rapture will start is when the trumpets will blow. The Lord, in the Bible, states that the trumpets will blow. We all believe it will be Gabriel blowing the trumpet. You will hear the trumpet blow even if you are in China or Alaska. Everyone will hear it blow. I sure want to be here when it blows.

The next thing that will take place is the Lord will say, "Come up hither, my children," and all who are saved and going to heaven will go with the Lord into the clouds. I told Jesus I could not wait; I want to be on the first load. (Giggles.) The Lord said, "No, Son, you do not want to be on the first load up. You want to be on the second load that comes up." Then of a sudden, without the Lord telling me anything else, it came to me. I have read the book of Thessalonians maybe two or three hundred times. It states the dead in Christ will rise first and that we who remain alive will meet them in the clouds. I know there must be ten to twenty million in the ocean who have been drowned by liberty ships and soldiers being sunk, and let us not forget the *Titanic*. I said, "Yes, Lord."

I said, "I want to go up on the second load, because the dead in Christ rise first, Lord, and we who remain and alive on earth will meet them in the clouds." You do have to be saved, though. Not everyone will go. I have read the book of Revelation forward one hundred times and backward over a hundred times. I memorized all the good parts in it word by word, comma for comma.

When the rapture takes place is when you will meet the Lord in the clouds. A lot of people say, "Well, if the dead go first, how long will it be before we go up to the clouds to meet the Lord?" No one truly knows—it could be a second or five or even minutes or day—but when it does happen, all who will go will be blessed. The rapture is when you lose all gravity, and no matter where you are, if you are saved, you will go up to meet the Lord.

A long time ago, they even had autopilots on planes. If you are a real safe pilot, or did not care too much about the Lord, they put you there. They had five or six hosts and at least four hundred passengers. What would happen is they knew if something would happen to the plane. I have been on big planes going to China, and maybe three hundred people would leave the plane. You would have a little over a hundred people left on the plane, and maybe two hostesses, and then the hostess would announce, "Well, the pilots are gone, but the plane is on autopilot." Then she would ask, "Is there anyone here who can sing, 'Amazing Grace'?"

We would have one of the ministers say, "I can lead everyone in 'Amazing Grace.'"

After around two or three hours, we started to run out of gas, and the hostess came back and said, "Everyone, fasten your seatbelts."

You have no clue where you're going to be during the rapture. You may be over an ocean or country or who knows. The host then will ask, "Is there anyone here who knows 'Nearer My God to Thee'?"

That's what's going to happen with the rapture. There's going to be coast guards, state police, army, navy, air force, and phone people. Everyone who is saved will go up to the heavens to meet the Lord, so there will be no services down here. When you are traveling down some of the roads anywhere in the world, you will see cars, trucks, and buses left stopped right in the middle of the roads or even maybe turned over, because all those people were the ones who went up to the heavens to meet the Lord. This is just a brief story about what will take place during the rapture.

The tribulation, the first forty-two months, of being up in heaven will not be too bad, but the last 42 months is when the antichrist will walk into the temple and claim, "I am God and everyone has to worship me, take the mark of the beast in your hand or forehead, 666." That's when, as the expression goes, all hell will break loose. We have all heard that.

I will just tell you this briefly. There is going to be a famine. People will not have enough to eat, and if you have even a loaf of bread, believe me, you will have something very, very valuable. A guy will come up to someone and say, "I just bought a new Cadillac for myself and my wife a new Towncar. I will trade you them both for that loaf of bread."

The person will laugh and say, "Sir, I surely do not know how a Cadillac or a Towncar would taste, but I do know how my loaves of bread taste."

You see, it is going to be such a famine, and people are not going to have enough food. This is just a little suggestion from this old preacher; I will tell you what you can eat. This will be the most healthy, nutritious thing you can eat, and you guessed it: **grass!** *Look at all the farm animals.* That is all they eat, and they are strong and healthy. When I was a young boy, there was many fields around my house there where these Italian women would take a knife, go out to the fields there, cut the dandelions greens, and take them home and make stew with them. I guess it kind of tasted like spinach. I never ate spinach and don't like spinach, but I will say that it is good for you and very healthy. I suggest you eat a lot of grass; it looks like I will have to learn to like it too.

It is going to be as the Bible says; there will be different unpleasant things will take place beside the famine. Plagues will take place, for example. It will also get hot—very hot. I have been in the desert in Cairo, Egypt, where its gets to be about 130 degrees. That is not too bad. I don't know for sure how hot it will be, but the Bible states people will be scorched, so it may be 160 or 170 degrees; now that's hot. The next thing that is going to happen is you're going have a bug, like a locust, and it's going to bite the people just like a scorpion. The sting is going to last for five months. Can you imagine what it will be like to be bitten by a scorpion and have the sting hurt and last for five months? It goes on and on and tells us the different plagues that will happen, and men will be so disgusted with God and curse God and call him a no-good, rotten person for doing this to them. They will take all their gold and umber with it. It says in the Bible that they will not repent; no matter what, they will not repent.

The Bible says one of the last things that will happen (this is all in Revelation, in case you like to know) is that there will be hailstones. Before there were refrigerators, we had ice men who would come with a delivery big blocks of ice (twenty-five pounds). If most of the ice melted, he would give you fifty pounds. They were around eighteen inches wide and twenty inches high and about a foot in a half thick. It says in the Bible a hail stone will be the weight of a tallit, which is one hundred pound. Wow, imagine having ice cubes coming down by tens and thousands and weighing about one hundred pounds apiece. This is really going to be one of the last straws.

According to the Bible, one of the seven things that will take place before the Lord comes back to earth is that the Armageddon War will happen. It has already taken place, with Iran and Libya. In the Bible, it states that first two countries will attack Jerusalem, and Libya has already attacked them; they have shown a lot bombs already going there. Iran was not called Iran back in 1930s; it was called Persia. In 1935 is when they had changed it. The Prince of Persia all through the Bible is the devil, so the Prince of Persia is Iran and is the devil. They have shown on national TV that every

Jew has to be completely eliminated from the face of the earth, and then they say the Americans are the ones helping the Jews because we are the ones sending them so many millions of dollars every day for equipments, parts, and things of that nature. This is why he hates the Americans.

During the time when the Armageddon War is going to take place, that will be the last war to take place. We always say that this war is the last war. The First World War was called the war to end all wars. The last war will be the Armageddon War, and this war will end all the wars. This war will make all the other wars look like a Sunday picnic. Half of the people on planet earth, according to the Bible, are going to be killed. I figure that at this time, there are at least six billion people living. The believers will be taken up into heaven. Then we will have the seven-year tribulation where more people will be born, so give or take a few billion, I figure half of six billion people is three billion. That will be a lot of dead people laying around. Now what happens is Zechariah 14:12. This verse tells you what is going to happen to all the people who attack Jerusalem.

I have told this verse, Zechariah 14:12, to many people, and most of them say, "I do not believe that. I do not remember reading or seeing that."

Therefore, what I do is open the Bible up and hand it to whoever and say, "Please read it aloud."

They would read it aloud themselves and the part where it reads, "And all the eyeballs will fall out," they go, "Oh Lord, *wow.*" Then they go on, and it states,

"Your tongues will fall out of your mouths, and your flesh is going to fall off while you are standing." These people are going to be in bad shape, I would say. This is all because of the nuclear bomb; the Lord knew when he wrote the Bible, that this would happen. He knew that people were going to develop the nuclear bomb, and it really does not hurt brick buildings too much, but as for the human race, well, that is another subject.

There will be billions of people with flesh falling off their bodies, tongues falling out of their mouths, and eyeballs popping out. Many people ask the question, "What are they going to do with all the bodies lying around?" It says four times in the Bible that the Lord will bring in these big birds, which I have seen in Jerusalem. They are called the carrion birds. They look like huge vultures. These birds have about a ten-foot wingspan, and they're big, huge birds. When I was in Jerusalem, I saw thousands of them. Their wingspans would block the sun right out. Therefore, the Lord will have these carrion birds come down and eat these people.

I said to the Lord, "Do you know how many of these birds you are going to need?"

The Lord said to me, "Son, you just do not know how many of the carrion birds I have."

You have seen all the bugs, fish, and birds we have now, so it will be no problem for the Lord to have enough carrion birds. That is what is going to happen with the Armageddon War. After the Armageddon War is over, it says the only way it will be over is that the Prince of Peace—who is Jesus—will come to end this Armageddon War. Who is coming with him? In the book of Revelation, it says the saints. The saints are coming back to reign and rule. Praise the Lord. There will be no more politicians, lobbyists, graft money under the table, extortion, or big paid vacations. The saints are going to rule this world, and it is going to be run right. The saints are coming back, and that is in the back part of the book of Revelation if you would like to read about it. What is going to happen is we are coming back here for one thousand years. In the millennium, which means a thousand years, believers come back for the thousand-year reign.

This is what I believe. We have governors now in different states, and they have a lot of power, but Jesus is the King of Kings and the Lord of Lords. I believe instead of having what we have now a governor of Florida, or any other state, there will be king of Florida or every other state. The kings are going to have better relationship with the people because the power will be given to him by Jesus, not the congress or senate, to run this place. With all of my talking with the Lord, I had to ask him if I would be the king of Florida. The Lord has not yet given me an answer, but I still have hopes that I will be the king of Florida.

It has been said that the oldest man to roam the earth with Jesus was Methuselah. You've heard people say, "You're as old as Methuselah." But others believe that the oldest man to roam the earth with Jesus is to be Enoch. The definition of Methuselah is, "When he is dead, it shall come." If we are going to be down here for one thousand years, we are going to have what the Lord calls a glorified body. He is not going to say to me,

"Brother Lee, go get some pain pills or false teeth." *No!* When the Lord fixes our bodies up, they will last a thousand years.

One thing I always disagree with the Lord about, and I'm sure there are many out there who agree with me, is that after the thousand years comes a judgment—you know, where everyone gets on their knees, every son must bow, every knee must bend and confess to Jesus Christ the Lord. Nevertheless, the Bible says that before the thousand years is when an angel takes a chain, ties it around the devil, and puts him the bottomless pit. This is why things are to be so nice for the thousand years. However, after the thousand years is up, the angel goes down to the devil and looses him.

I say to the Lord, "Take that sun of a gun into the lake of fire."

The Lord tells me, "That's right, my son, you read the book. That's where the devil is going into the lake of fire, along with all the disbelievers, and Athens, and the cult believers, people who don't worship God at all. They all will go into the lake of fire."

I said to the Lord, "Why don't you put them in there right away and not let him loose to cause more trouble?"

Now the big answer to that is if everything is going smooth for thousand years, with no devil or no problems, those people will not be confronted with the devil, as we are now. The Lord says, "It would be sort of justice for those who have had the devil on their back all this time and for these people not to."

Now this is just a theory, and I would like to make this clear, that this in not in the Bible, but what people of the years have been saying.

This is the millennium and what I have talked to the Lord about. We do not know how old we're going to be when we do come back to get this glorified body. I believe that when we do come back to get this glorified body, we will be, or I should say I believe we will be, the same age as Jesus when he rose from the grave. This will be thirty-three and a half years old. I've talked with Jesus so many times, and I say, "Jesus, if I'm going to come back thirty-three and a half years old, at that time I only looked like I was about twenty-seven. That's why I could go out with these young girls. They thought I was younger than I appeared. Lord, here's what I would love for you to do; I would love for you to create the most beautiful woman you have every created with the most beautiful long legs, eyes, and hairs, and very romantic, seeing that I am a very romantic preacher. But she must love the Lord the way I do."

I've never had any children, but I would have loved had two beautiful girls, one for each knee, the way they sat on Jesus knees. I would ask my daughters, "Have you two been good to Mother today?"

They would say, "Oh yes, yes, Daddy. We have been very good."

I would ask my daughters, "Would you like Daddy to take you both for Big Mac and French fries today?"

"Oh yes, Daddy!"

I would say, "Okay, give Daddy a kiss.

I always thought this would be one of the greatest pleasures a man could ever have, to have a couple beautiful little girls. Next to the church building where I live, there were two little girls; one was around four and the other around two. They were the cutest and sweetest little girls in the world. They would cuddle up and look up at me with their big eyes and smile. Oh, it just made my heart melt. I would tell their mother and father that they are the luckiest people in the world to have such beautiful, wonderful little girls. I said to the Lord, "If I am to have a gorgeous woman in my life, well instead of two daughters, why not seven beautiful daughters? That is not too many to have in a thousand years. Oh yes and a couple of sons. A man always wants a son."

My biggest desire in the world is to be in the rapture, to lose all gravity, and fly right up there with Jesus and then to be able to come back and have the family I truly want. My second wish I have is that the book I am writing gets out for all the world to have and read.

I want children and people to read about Jesus. The Bible states he is the same yesterday and today and forever. Well, if you read the Bible, you know what he did and the future; that is in the book of Revelation and Thessalonians. You will find out what he will do in the future, but this is what he did today. I watch TV and all people who write books. They start out with one subject that happens in their life, and that is all the book is about. Here in this book, I will talk about dozens and dozens and dozens of miracles that have taken place all over the world. I have laid my hands over millions of God's children and have prayed for every one I have touched who wanted to be healed and who was looking for a miracle.

When I watch TV, these people are writing books and making money! The best books on the New York bestseller list are books that address questions like: Is there really a God? Is there really a Jesus? Is he a man, or is he a saint? Did he really exist? Did he really do miracles? Some of these are written by priests and bunch of others are written by college professors. I will not tell you the ones the Lord told me about that are the worst colleges in the state; I will not belittle anyone, but he said some of these children who are in the colleges today are brought up Christians and are taught, "Jesus loves me, this I know, for the Bible tells me so." Their mothers took them to Sunday school and everything; then when they go to college, the professor tells them that's all a bunch of hogwash. We will not be talking about Jesus here; that's against the law, and we are here to teach you the real truth, all about evolution, and the books you're going to read will be about evolution.

If that teacher wants to go to *hell,* that is his own business. He is entitled to go to *hell,* but he is going to end up taking many college students with him, because they will believe him. I have been to heaven to be with the Lord, and I would love to take as many as I can with me. These professors and others are teaching the wrong thing. They know nothing of the Lord. If they could have seen or would have been part of the miracles, all I want to do is be the Lord's servant. I'm awful humble to be his servant, and I'm more proud than ever to just be his sidekick. The Lord just told me I am his sidekick because he's the one who gave me my nose and toes and heart beats, and he did the same to all of those who teach the wrong things about our Lord. When it comes time for them to get on their knees on the judgment stand, there are only two sentences that the Lord is going to command. When you are on your knees, your big fanny will be sticking out; there will be no clothes or anything of that nature.

The Bible states you came into this world with nothing; you didn't come into this world with a diaper on and you're going out the same way you came into the world, with not a stitch of clothing on. What the Lord is going to say is, "Here is beloved son in whom I'm well pleased." He died for you and shed his blood for you, and down on planet earth, you didn't want to be involved with the Lord. Now you're up here and now you want to be involved with the Lord! Well what makes you think he wants to be involved with you now? You never wanted to be involved with the Lord before. You had many chances and never stood up for him, the man who gave you your eyes, ears, nose, mouth, heart, and toes. You were ashamed!

The Bible says that if you're ashamed down in that wicked world to stand up for God's Son, when you get in front of me God your knees, the Lord will be ashamed of you! There are only two sentences the Lord knows when you are on your knees! The first one is, *"My good and faithful servant, enter in!"* (Wow!) Everybody is going to want to hear that, but how could you be a good and faithful servant when you wanted no part of the Lord, let alone to be involved with him? A nine-year-old even knows that the Lord not going to tell you to enter in. The second one is, *"Depart from me, I never knew you!"*

I make a little joke about this one. I say if you do not like that decision, you tell him right there. You have got him right there and he is the source. You can say, "I've got some good corporate attorneys, and I'm going to take this to a higher court, and if I have to, I'll take it to the supreme court," Giggles, "and I have some attorneys who can get me all the appeals I want," (giggling). Brother, you are at the supreme court! This is the court where there are no appeals. There is no court higher. Now when the sentence is read, *"Depart from me, I never knew you,"* that's it; that is the end. I hope this never happens to anybody who reads this book. I want everyone to be saved. I have talked to over twenty thousand people on my front porch and held their hands, so that means on the front porch alone, I've held forty thousand hands, and I have prayed for them. Out of the forty thousand, you just can't imagine all the wonderful miracles I have seen and people came back and talked with me. I didn't even know they had their miracle. I have gotten many letters that say things like, "When you prayed for me brother." They tell me all the wonders that they had happen and thank me so much.

Praise the Lord.

If you read the book of Revelation, it does tell you the final trip you are going to take. The final trip is in the *Lake of Fire!* When it has says all people that are not called, *"Enter in, my good and faithful servant,"* they are taken to the Lake of Fire with the devil and the Antichrist. What happens in the lake of fire is that your flesh will be consumed. It won't be consumed by the fire. It will just keep on burning, not just for the weekend. It states that people will be gnashing their teeth, screaming, and yelling, and you will not be alone. That's one good things, because there will be billions of people there with you. Just imagine being in the Lake of Fire and being tormented like that and never ever getting out. That is what the consensus is going to be. The Lake of Fire and is the final thing in the book of Revelation, if he does not say, *"Enter in, my good and faithful servant,"* their destination will be the Lake of Fire.

Praise the Lord.

One of My Greatest Wishes

Before the rapture takes place, I, Preacher Man Lee, have a dream I would love to accomplish. You might ask what that dream is. It would give me great pleasure to travel all over the world to all of the veterans' hospitals. The very first veterans' hospital would be in Germany, because that is where they send most of the American boys, over there in Germany. I have seen on TV that most of them are in bad shape. They have no feet, legs, or arms, and some even have half a face. The next one would be in Hawaii; I was there maybe forty-some years ago. My point is I want to go to all of them all over the world, as I stated, because these are all of God's children, and they are young boys who just started life as we know it. Some of them even have wives and babies and have not even had the opportunity to see them. I think of how their lives have been cut so short and they have not even had the pleasure of life, let alone some of them being consecrated to the Lord.

The Lord and I talked about this, and he told me how to go about this. I have had a beautiful life with our Lord. This is my eighty-fourth year, and I have a wonderful life, with pools, cars, mansions, world travel, friends, and yes, my close and personal walk with the Lord. Therefore, it breaks my heart for these young men to have never even had the opportunity to live their life like that.

The Lord told me how to do this. I want to give out a number of books to these hospitals for them to read, and if they cannot read, I pray someone will read it to them. The thing is in my mind, and it has been in my mind for a long time, so I will tell it now. "Jesus the same yesterday, today, and forever."

If you read the Bible, you already know about Jesus' life from the time he was born until the time he died at thirty-three and a half years of age.

Then you can read the future. The book of Revelation or the book of Thessalonians it tells exactly what will happen after the Armageddon War, and it tells the complete future of your life.

Now what happens today, yesterday, now, and forever? The Lord wants his children to know what is happening today, the miracles he is doing, the things that are happening, and the things we can expect from him. That is why the Lord and I are writing this book. It tells everything he has been doing today.

Now when I go to the veterans' hospitals, what I would like to do is take many pictures of Jesus with me. I have beautiful pictures of Jesus walking on water, and it would give me great honor and joy to hand them out to all of them, like I do here now, to all of the Lord's children. In addition, I would love to have a red anointed prayer cloth for them.

The Lord said, "Son, when you go there, you make small talk about yourself, and then you tell them the Lord is coming and we're all getting ready for him, and we do not want any one left behind. Now you can tell them look when the Lord comes and takes us up to heaven (which we believe is coming soon), the Lord isn't going to say, 'Well, you have to get a new pair of teeth, or some better eyes, and those knees of yours that are worn out, from working so hard for the Lord.' A doctor says, 'You have no cartilage left in your knees.' *No!* The Lord is going to give us all a glorified body. The Lord asked me to come here and see you all and kiss your necks and feet and to let you know that the Lord is coming. You will have a glorified body, and if you want blond hair or short hair or if you want to be a certain height, you just tell the Lord."

I make a little joke and say to the Lord, "Most of my friends are taller than me, and they call me short. If you can give me another three inches, Lord, that will help." Whatever you want, the Lord will give you. Now when I tell them this, it will give them faith of what has to come soon. Many of these young men have probably not even had visitors or anyone to come and see them.

Therefore, this is my last dream in life that I wish to do. It will give me pleasure to talk to them. I have talk to the Lord every night of how I want to go see all of them. I would love when the rapture took place, I was with some of the Veterans', and up they went with me. In the book of Thessalonians, it states

"The dead in Christ will rise first and we that remain in our lives will meet them in the clouds."

I cannot stress enough that this is my biggest dream. As I wrote this book, I shared all the tears with the Lord.

Praise the Lord.

Give Pictures of Jesus Walking on Water
I Tried It Myself

One of my very favorite pastimes, or I should say hobbies, has been taking pleasure in giving out pictures of Jesus walking on water. I had a picture of the same in a frame and knew how much I enjoyed looking at it, so I decided if I love looking at it so very much, and have tried for years myself to walk on water in the beautiful lakes and my swimming pool in Florida, I wanted to share the picture with all of the Lord's children.

In one of my tapes, I mentioned I could walk on water, but it had to be up in Michigan where is cold. Then I could walk or skate on it. In addition, when on my sailboat, I was always asking and hoping that Jesus would walk on the water and come in the sailboat with me to talk with me. At this point, you can see how much I enjoyed having the beautiful pictures of Jesus on my desk.

It came to me that if I enjoyed this picture so much, so would many more people, and immediately I had the great idea for giving them out to as many people as possible. In a heartbeat, the next idea came to me. I certainly could not charge for giving away the beautiful picture of Jesus and could not stand the terrible thought of selling them. Anyway, I went to a printer and had about fifty made up. Wow, was I happy. Now I had fifty pictures of Jesus walking on water.

I started to give them out in different stores or in lines at supermarkets. Often donations were offered for the pictures, but I always said, "I am sorry. I cannot take a donation for my Savior's picture."

Soon the fifty pictures were gone, and my best friend and member of the board of directors at the chapel told me he had a computer and could print them for me. I said, "Wonderful, we can get them out cheaper and a lot more of them." He told me to go to a large department store and get the ink and printing paper, and he would start getting them out. I am obedient, so off I went.

The paper was about $20 back then. I went to the ink department, and they had two little bottles on a card. I decided to buy that, and the clerk said, "That will be $64." Wow, that is about $84 in all. Well, if that is the way it is, that is the way it is. I do not care about cost. We had to get Jesus walking on water, and the blessings I received were worth the price.

One happy day, I gave out a picture (the pictures are eight-by-ten glossies on heavy paper). I told the recipient she could get a gold frame for $2. Another girl, about seventeen, who I gave a picture to about two weeks earlier said she put coracles all around it and prays to Jesus every night. What a blessing for me to hear all the wonderful compliments from all I have given the picture to.

My brother Bill, who prints them out on his printer, is more than sharing the cost. I estimate I have given away approximately two thousand copies around the city. Everywhere I go, I have my folder with me and full at all times. We also give one to each family that visits the Jesus Miracle Chapel. Many times, I have offered a picture and the recipient would say, "Oh, you gave me one of those about two months ago." I also have people who say, "Isn't it beautiful? I know my mother and brother would love one, and I would be glad to buy two or three more from you." I tell them I sure hope they enjoy them and that makes my day, and I want them to enjoy the at-no-charge compliments from Jesus. I have so many more stories I could tell you, but that gives you some idea of the great pleasure it has given me and Big Bill, who prints them out for Jesus and me.

Praise the Lord.

Calling God Father

This is a little story that will interest a lot of folks and maybe shock you. Listen to my first statement. It will make you so much happier like I am.

Father God sat down alongside of me on the sofa. I could feel his presence, and naturally, I did not see him. Father God started to tell me, "Son, you and I have such a wonderful relationship, you, my son, my spirit, and I. My son, I would love to keep the relationship you and I have, but I would like to improve it. This is what I suggest to you. Instead of you calling me God, I would prefer you call me Father."

"Wow!" I replied. I have called him Father and Father God, but he wants me to call him Father, so I call him Father now. This has done so much for me in the past. This has happened within the last seven or eight months before this book was finished.

I have a very close friend who is a doctor and has seen many miracles. He has been to my home to visit me on several occasions. We sit and talk about the world, Bible, and many other subjects. Peter and I would pray together, and I always call him Doc. Jesus knows us all by our first names. One night we were having service, and I told him to say the Lord's Prayer in Greek. Then the two of us would say the Lord's Prayer in English. This wonderful Christian man sitting alongside of me, I had told him what Father had told me to call him, and said, "Why isn't that peculiar? Just around the

184

same time Father told you that, he told me the same thing. Wow, this is just wonderful. We will both call him Father."

I must call him Father at least fifty times a day or more. Father this, let's go shopping or cut the grass. Ever since this, it has made a more closer and personal walk and talk with our Savior (*Father*). My father passed away when I was around four and a half years old, so I really never had a father, so this is such a true blessing for me to have such a close relationship with our Savior. Before I go to bed, I always tell Father to have a good night and his Son.

If it is good for this remarkable preacher to call him Father, then why don't the rest of us take him for his word and start calling him Father? We all need a closer and personal walk with our Savior.

After that, I have been trying to figure it out why he would want me to call him Father. I had the Holy Spirit come to me and help me with this. The Holy Spirit and I came up with the conclusion that there are so many different gods in this word, and that the true Lord only wants to be called Father. All of these others are those like the rain gods and sun gods, and there are others who toss live babies off high cliffs. Then there are the Pegasus gods. *No*, there is one Holy Father, and that is it. More and more churches are not saying, "Happy Easter" anymore, due to it being Pegasus. Now they are saying, "Happy Resurrection Day."

If you look back in history, different countries had many different gods, so when we say God now, it just doesn't have that very close meaning at all for our True Savior, Father. This is the reason I believe he wants me and the rest of us to call him Father.

Praise the Lord.

Preacher Kisses Jesus Mother's Hands

I Rev. Lee and Mary went up to paradise, and not many can go up to the heavens to have the glory and pleasure to see our creator, and meet his mother, the Mother Mary.

Mother Mary was standing about 18" to my left of me, and I looked at Mother Mary first, then I glanced over at Jesus, and I said, well there's another Mary here, and my exact words were how do you like that.

I walked right in front of Mother Mary, and she was at least a foot in half, and I looked right into her eyes, and I notice her skin, she has such a remarkable glow to her, not a lot but enough that I did take notice of it. There was no blemish on her face it was just white and pure as could be. I wanted to grip her right away and give her the biggest bear hug, but there was something inside me and the spirit said no, you don't grab Jesus mother and give her a big bear hug. I looked at her and took her two hands and raised them up to my mouth, and I took the back of her hands, and kissed them three times. This gave me so much honor and grace to do this. Then I had turned around and the other Mary, my dearest closest friend whom took the time to type this book for myself and our creator. Mary was standing next to Jesus, and Jesus had on his Gold Lamay outfit. I Lee have prayed 365 nights every year for over 30 years, which I recall, to have the privilege and honor to see Jesus in his Gold Lamay outfit. I have seen Jesus many times, but never in his gold outfit, and on this night to have my dearest friend Mary with me to see

Jesus and Mother Mary, what a true blessing this was. Jesus put his arms around me and gave me the bear hug. What a pure feeling for Jesus to give myself and Mary the pleasure to see and meet him and Mother Mary.

Praise The Lord

Preachers

I have had the privilege of working with most of the well-known preachers out there. It gives me great pleasure and honor to mention them:

- Billy Graham
- Paul Crouch
- R. W. Schambach
- W. V. Grant Jr.
- Richard Hall
- Kenneth Hagin
- George Callahan

If I forgot anyone, Father, forgive me. I love you all, and thank you so much.

I have been on many stages with these preachers, and I have learned so much from them all. I just want to thank them. I truly wish I could remember them all, but these are a few I do remember. I hope and pray that all of these preachers continue to pray and have wonderful services with all of Father's children.

I hope to see you all in heaven with me, so we can all sit down together with Jesus and break bread once again.

May the Lord be with us all.

Amen.

The Miracle of the Red Cloth

I have handed out thousands of red cloths, and if you believe, miracles will happen. A young man came up to me at the store and asked if I would pray for him. I handed him a red cloth and told him to rub it all over his body. Not just any piece of red cloth will work. A red cloth has to be blessed and anointed before you lay it on your parts you want healed, or you may lay it under your pillow at night time. This young fellow had tumors and was told he didn't have much time, so I had the anointed red cloth and prayed for him, and he took the red cloth. When he saw me again, he could not wait to tell me he had been healed, and even all of the doctors could not believe their eyes. This is just another wonderful miracle I wanted to tell you all again.

Remember, if you desire an anointed red prayer cloth, you can contact me by mail. Send your request of what you need with a self-addressed envelope, and I will send you back your anointed prayer cloth, which will be prayed on for whomever needs it. I have had several come back for more prayer cloths to pass on to others. Send your requests to:

Pastor Lee Hoffman
Jesus Miracle Chapel
9090 E. Bronson Highway
St. Cloud, Florida, 34773

Praise the Lord.

Pastor Lee Hoffman
Hand Built the Sign
"Jesus Miracle Chapel"

Millions of More Thank Yous from Jesus

I live in a little town called Holopaw, Florida, near Saint Cloud, Florida. I go to town nearly every day to do my shopping and to stop at one of my favorite fast food places to get me and Jesus a taco. When I tell people that I'm going into town to do this, they get such a chuckle out of it. I remember one time I was just sitting down to thank the Lord for my food. I was about to eat when a little nice grandma came up to me, and she had her grandchildren with her. She came up to me and said, "I just couldn't believe my eyes. I never before have seen anyone sit down and give thanks like that before they eat. It just brought a tear to my eyes, with me here with my grandchildren. Sir, you have just taught me a good lesson." We all said a little prayer, and like I have done over and over, I gave the grandchildren a photo of Jesus walking on water and a million-dollar bill with a depiction of Jesus on it. The little girl smiled and told me she was going to put the picture of Jesus in a frame.

If you pray before you eat, you will be a happier person. Remember to inspire to aspire before you expire. Keep our Creator in your heart and mind at all times.

Lee Hoffman

Just a Few Short Subjects from Lee and Father God

Father and I were sitting up by the church, and we were talking about the Lord's Supper. He went in to detail of how he wanted me to take the Lord's Supper and where I am to touch myself. It gives me great pleasure and honor to share it with all of Jesus' children.

First are the healing and the drinking of the wine. When you take the wafer or the bread, you chew it thirty-nine times. This represents, the stripes on Jesus' back. This is for the healing. Now when you anointed yourself with the olive oil, which is very holy, take your left hand and place it on the top of your head and ask Lord to build up your immune system. This is, of course, when you apply the oil.

The Lord said, "When you leave your house and get in your car, put both hands on top of your hand and spiritually cover yourself with the blood of Jesus." There are so many people who are drunk drivers or speeding and playing on their phones, so please spiritually anoint yourself.

Whenever you are fixing things around your house, car, whatever it may be, don't be afraid to ask Jesus for help. Say, "Jesus, I don't need your help right just now, I need your help all the time, but right now I truly do need your help." Jesus has helped me on so many different occasions. Thank you.

Praise the Lord.

Last Two Verses of the Bible
The Final Word

I would like to give a little joke first, and then I thought to myself, *Well, I don't want to step on anybody's toes.* I talked to the Lord, and he told me, "You go right ahead, my son. This is how I want you to end the book with the last two verses of the Bible."

The Lord said, "I am the way of truth and life. No one goes to the Father expect through me."

I replied to the Lord, "Hey, now that's good Lord. I've said that thousands of times to thousands of people. Okay, Lord, what's the next one?"

The Lord answered, "There is no other name, under heaven given among men, whereby we must be saved."

"Hey," I tell the Lord, "now that is almost like the first one.

The Lord replied, "Yes, my son, this is the way the book should end."

Thank you, readers.

Praise the Lord.

Pastor Lee Hoffman and Mary Stauffer

Jesus and I would like to take this time to thank Mary for all the time and work she has put into this book for all of the Lord's children to read.

May the Lord be with you all and your families. *Amen.*

Favorite Verse

I know the world's most favorite verse is John 3:16. You see this in the ball park or football stadium. My favorite verses that have stuck with me are Mark 8:36–37, which say:

> *For what shall if profit a man, if he shall gain the whole world, and lose his own soul?* Or what shall a man give in exchange for his soul?

I have this on my vehicle, and people shake my hand for this saying on my car.

I asked Jesus about these two verses, and I thought I knew what it meant, but I wanted to hear it from Jesus. It means everything in this whole world, gold and silver and everything. Jesus wanted to come on in a strong verse.

Praise the Lord.

The Anointing Breaks the Yoke

We all have various kinds of problems: marriage, financial, health, children, etc. In the Book of James (King James Version of the Bible) a true brother of Mary said to use oil in the anointing of a person, and with the prayers of the elders of the church. By doing this the ill person would recover.

Anointing with oil is not something somebody just made up – the use of oil for anointing appears over and over again in the Bible.

A true brother of Mary, Jude, would do this. He was the person that wrote the Book of Jude, which appears in the Bible next to the book of Revelation.

The Bible tells a story about a wonderful anointing – Aaron, a highly appointed person that was Moses' right hand man and helper, mentioned this in the book of Exodus (King James Version of Bible).

One day, a long time ago, as we were having our annual Jesus Miracle Chapel Board meeting, Mr. Wiggalsworth's grandson was present. Mr. Wiggalsworth's father was a famous preacher who raised dead people. One man in particular was embalmed in a coffin in an old county church (there was no air conditioning, just open windows). Jesus told Mr. Wiggalsworth's son, "Get that man out of his casket."

The man came to life and the people started jumping out the windows of the church.

Another incidence – Mr. Wiggalsworth stood a dead person up against the wall and told him to live…*and* he lived.

People should buy Mr. Wigglesworth's books – they talk in more detail about the miracles he performed.

Mr. Wigglesworth's grandson at the Jesus Miracle Chapel Board Meeting anointed me with oil, so much oil that it ran over my head, pants, and into my tennis shoes. I didn't have a beard like Aaron had for it to run into.

Again, the anointing destroys the Yoke.

The Yoke is a person's problems; the oil breaks the yoke, or the problems, in an individual's life. The oil is Holy it lessens the person's problems. All of Jesus' disciples used oil in their anointing of people. All through the Bible it said they used olive oil for special anointing occasions.

When you pray, you're supposed to use anointing oil. James, Jesus' true brother from the Virgin Mary, who wrote the Book James, used anointing oil in his prayers.

If anybody ever asks you did Jesus ever have brothers, you could say yes. James and Jude, who wrote two books in the Bible, were their names. James and Jude like the names found in the New Testament.

I have given away hundreds and hundreds of bottles of anointing oil, put into little vitamin bottles. The people ask me what I do when the oil is used up. I told them to go get some olive oil, it's the same thing. And you can use this oil to anoint yourself when you say the Lord's Prayer.

A lot of preachers carry a little bottle of oil with them and when they pray they use this oil in context with their prayers on people.

Every night I take the oil and put it on my fingers, make a cross on my heart and say "I give you my heart so willingly, happily, and gladly," and then I make a cross on my forehead to do the work of God. I then do it again on my feet, to walk in the path of rightness all the days of my life. A lot of people came up to me and I anoint their left hand with oil and if they have cancer this will absolutely heal the cancer.

The Lord told me to do this on hundreds of people, make a little cross with oil on the left hand and say in the name of Jesus, Son of the Most High

God, We denounce this cancer in the name of Jesus; Cancer be gone! By the Authority of Jesus Christ.

I always anoint my tongue in the name of Jesus.

Spending an Hour with Jesus Makes a Very Happy Marriage

Everyone has 24 hours a day for themselves. Now what would happen if people would take one hour and give it to Jesus each day? This is what this section is about.

After spending a beautiful day doing the things you want to do, what you could do here, we've done it ourselves, and it is very successful, and people have come back to me and said so. Give your time to Jesus, at least one hour a day. The other 23 hours are yours.

I would like to dedicate this book to my Creator and Savior, the one who gave me my nose and toes. He made it possible for me to have this wonderful relationship with him and to be a witness to all of the amazing miracles I have seen. I would also like to thank my wonderful Christian mother, who taught me to be a great Christian man and made it possible for me to travel across the world and be called a preacher.